HOUSE & CONTENTS

HOUSE & CONTENTS

GREGORY O'BRIEN

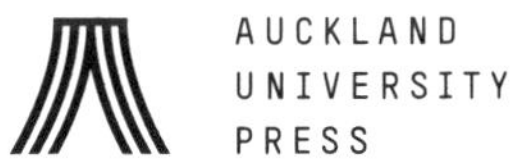

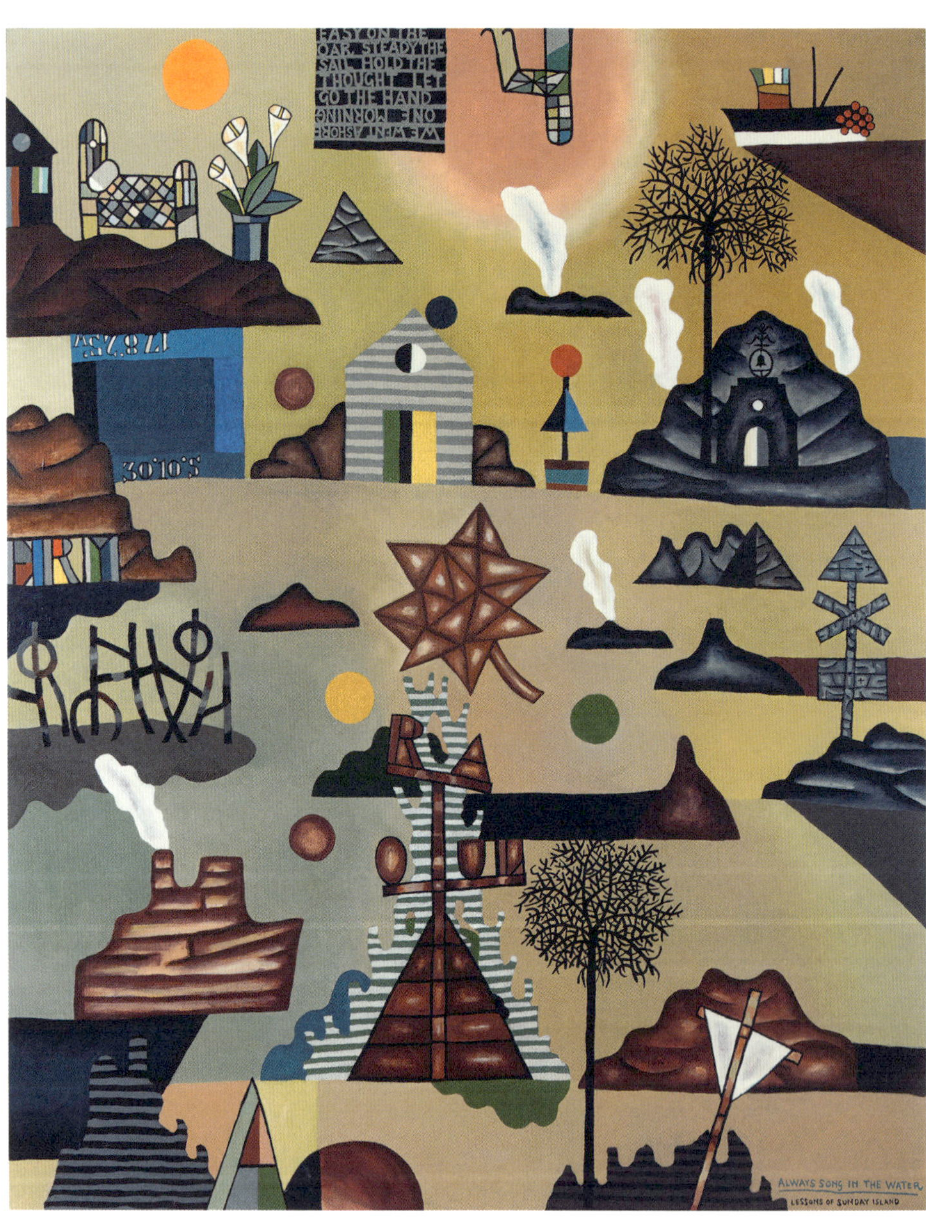
EASY ON THE
OAR STEADY THE
SAIL HOLD THE
THOUGHT LET
GO THE HAND
30°10'S
ALWAYS SONG IN THE WATER
LESSONS OF SUNDAY ISLAND

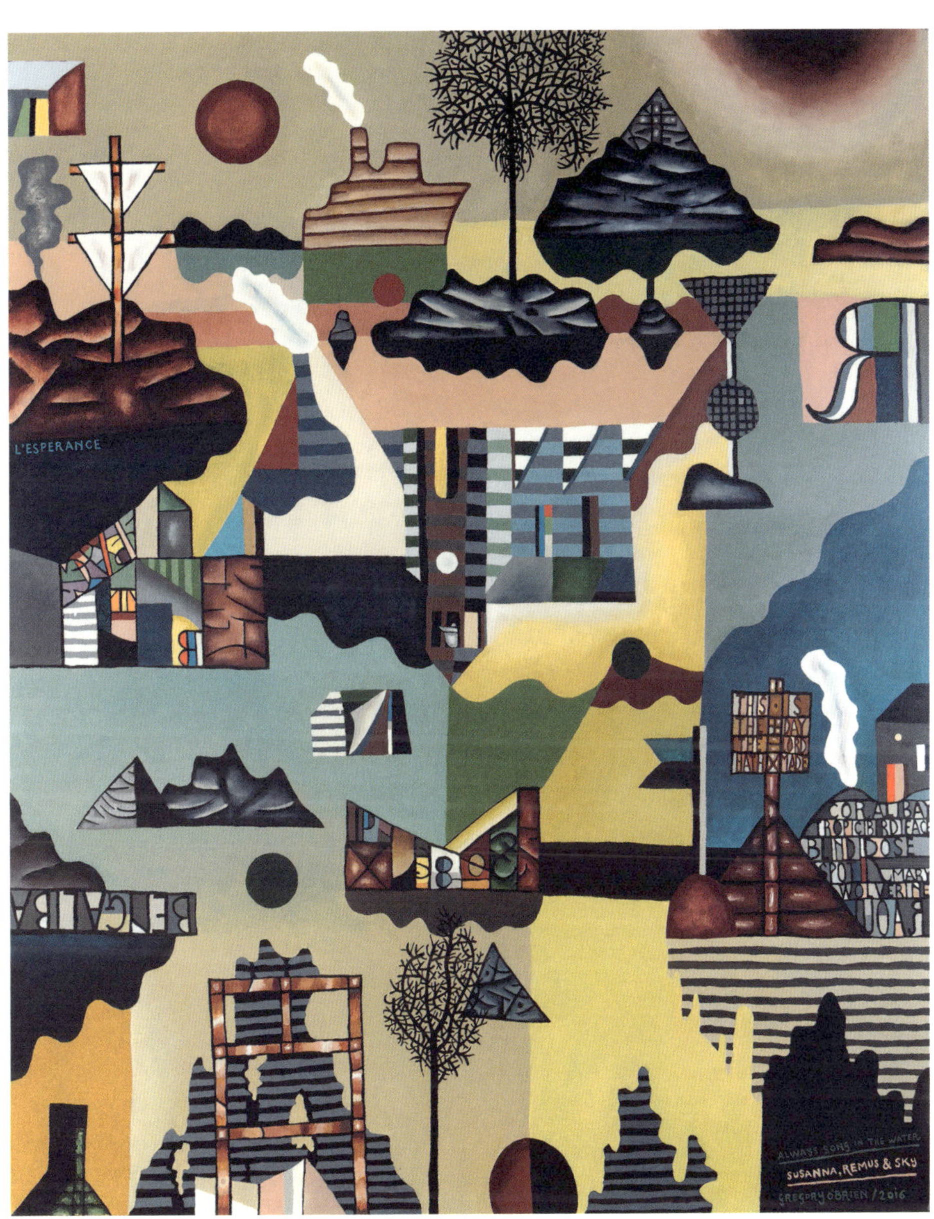
L'ESPERANCE
ALWAYS SONG IN THE WATER
SUSANNA, REMUS & SKY
GREGORY O'BRIEN / 2016

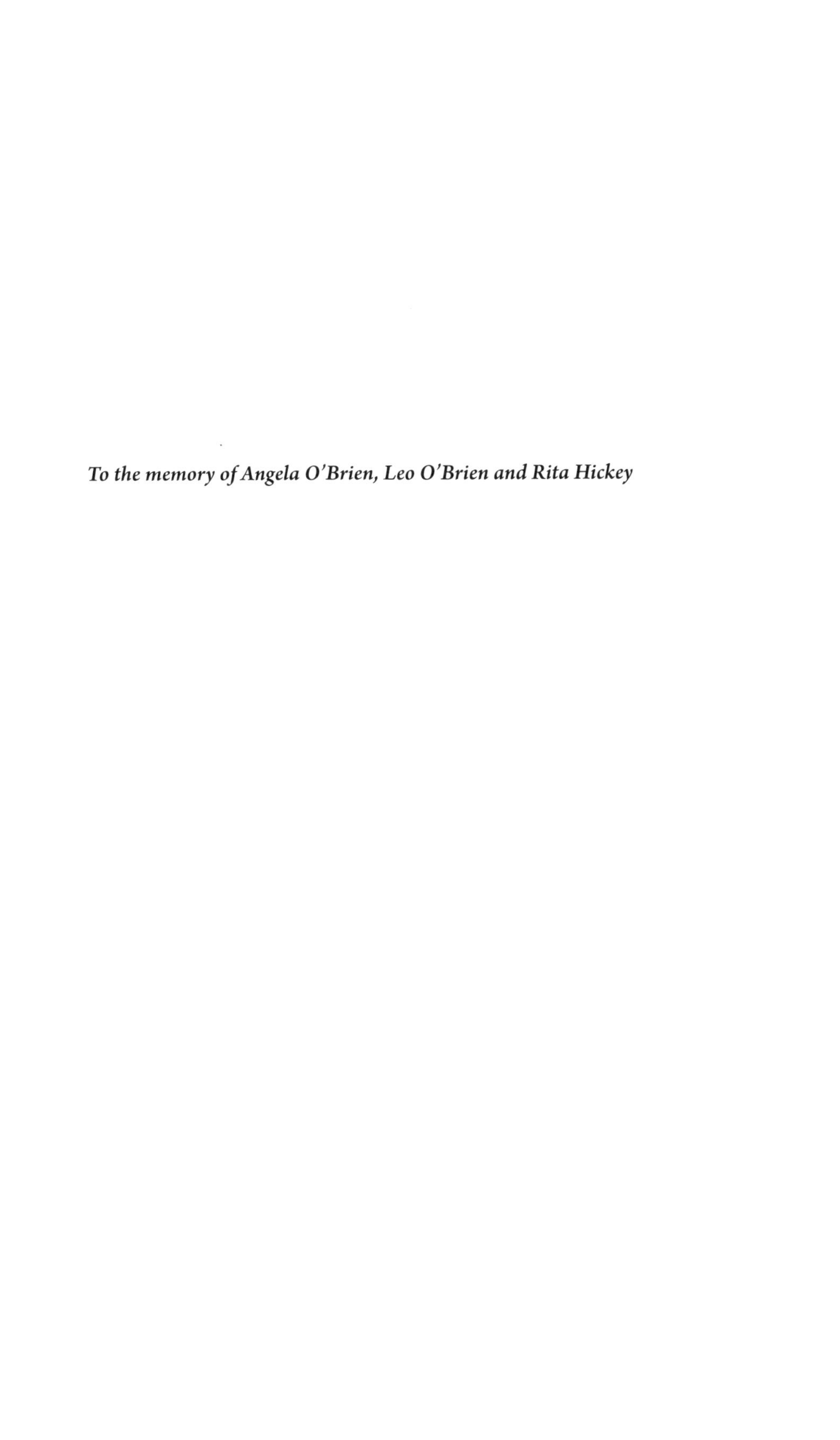

To the memory of Angela O'Brien, Leo O'Brien and Rita Hickey

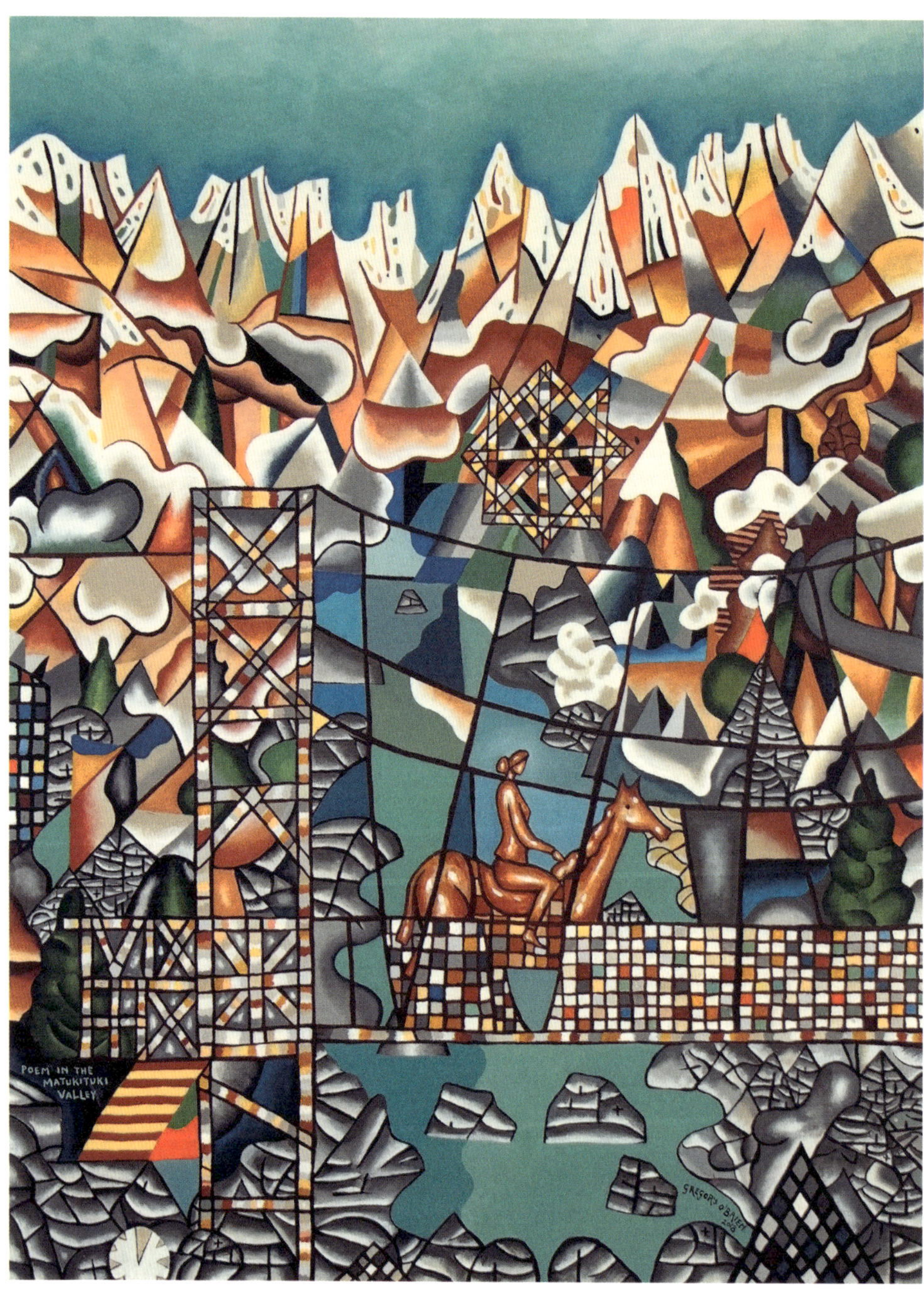
POEM IN THE
MATUKITUKI
VALLEY
GREGORY O'BRIEN

Mihi

The birds and animals of our mother's land greet
    the birds and animals of your land.
Her waterways, tributaries
and flooded plains
    greet yours. Now she is gone, she joins
the dead of her tribe
in greeting
    your dead. And her dead
birds and animals offer this, their heartfelt
address, to your dead birds, animals.

And to the living. Her constellations greet your
    constellations and if they happen to be
    the same constellations
they wrap their arms around
    themselves.
Her fruit trees, in season, greet
    your fruit trees, their fallen fruit.

Our mother's clouds and insects
    fly to embrace your clouds
and insects. Her architecture, roads,
bridges and infrastructure
    rush to greet yours.
Her molecules on their upward trajectory
entwine with yours, the colour of her eyes,
hair and skin. Her language,

with its past
participles, figures of speech,
    the sounds and tremors
which are its flesh and bones
these words go out
to greet your words and
    to greet you –
these words
which will never leave her.

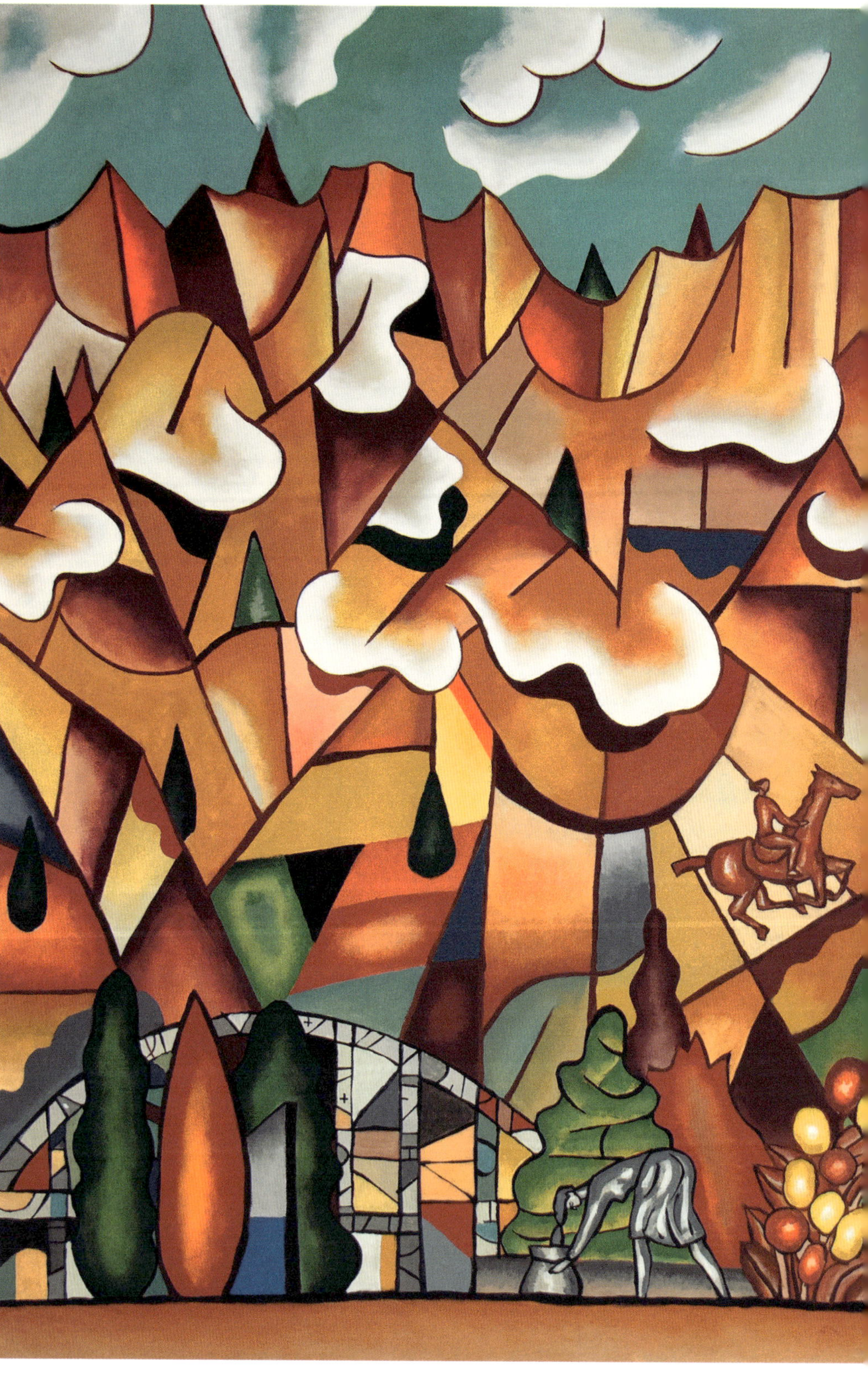

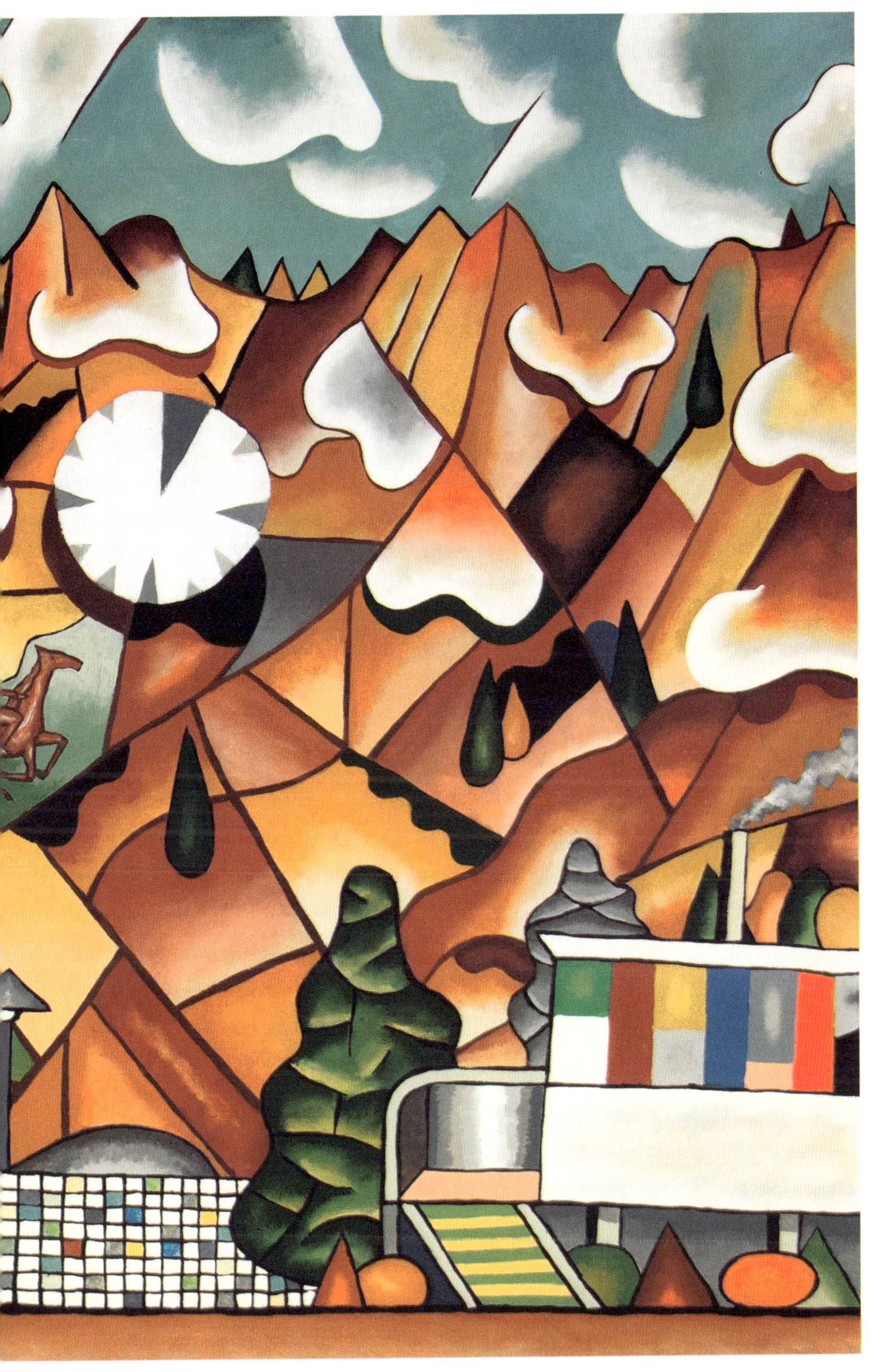

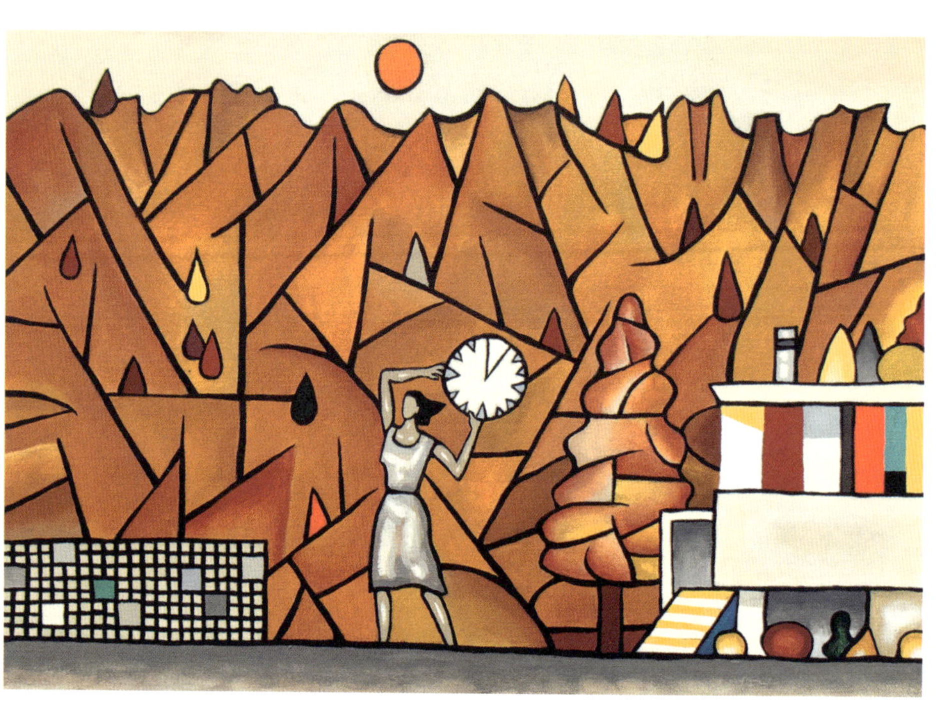

House and contents

Wellington, 20 August, 9am Sometimes the wooden beams, as they creak and contort, sound like voices. An occasional gasp. A cluck. A groaning. Sitting in the corner of a bedroom, I am listening to the house. It is three days since a 6.6 earthquake rocked Wellington and the earthquake cluster / swarm is still being felt.

On the afternoon of the first of the recent quakes – 21 July – I was standing on my sister-in-law's lawn when birds suddenly vacated the surrounding trees and began flying in unusual yet strangely preordained patterns; a dog curled up into a ball. Next thing, leaves on overarching branches began vibrating, lit up by a frenetic, other-worldly light. Then the trunks began to swivel and the ground to roll. By then, piles of bedside-books in the literary households of Wellington were tumbling, and, a short distance up the coast, a friend was standing in the middle of her living room, clutching her well-populated goldfish bowl, trying to stop the contents from emptying onto the floor, while all around her paintings were flying from the walls and glass was breaking.

House

A man or woman
might be remembered
as a house
          the living room
immense with their
breathing, the staircase

a spine, and the kitchen
          an ear listening to all
the other rooms; the study which is both

mind and elbow, the corridor
          an outstretched arm – and
what it holds in its palm:

childhood. Then the music room which is
every room, as music should always be
          every part
of a body. A house might also be remembered
for the synchronicity of
          its bedrooms, densely wooded eyes

or for its wiring – the brilliant circuitry
of a family, for it is the house
illuminates the tree outside, sheds
          its foliage
of electric light. And so

come evening, a dwelling is scattered
but not divided
          and, in daylight,
returned to itself –
a house that stands its ground, or must be
placed on that ground

as naturally as
fruit fallen
from a tree. So a life
is also laid down, and further,
to rest.

in memory of Frank Jones, architect, and his wife Pat

Te whakarite puāwai

Always they were someone's: Bob's daffodils, Mrs Henderson's rowan berries, Eric and Annemarie's dahlias, the Drivers' cottonwood and wheatgrass, Grahame's lavender (through which his blind dog Milo nuzzled its way, and beneath which he now sleeps), Fi's geraniums, the Bornholdt family's wild asparagus lawn, Tim's creeping herb and alpine carrot, Gillian's mixed salad pasture.

Firstly, it was seabirds led them inland, upriver – oystercatchers of the Lindis Stream, wading birds of Drybread – amidst edelweiss and whipcord scrub, Loretta's rare native cress, an assortment of saltgrass and sedge, Andrew's scree buttercup, Ernst Plischke's untameable olearia, shrubby broom and kākā beak. Samples were taken, as a garland: for Brian, saltgrass and common thyme; for Sam, hard tussock and woollyhead.

But it was the flowering that held them, as specimens in their own box seat or Wardian case, year by year gathered and groomed, watched over by rare climber and twiggy coprosma, conspicuous moss and speargrass, in their late summerhouse, their temporary pavilion.

for Mark Smith and Felicity Jones

Father

'Buried at sea, yesterday.'
(Epitaph for John Patrick O'Brien, as requested)

How far from where you are to where
I am, both of us
dusted off, shirts

pressed, trousers adjusted. These songs being
such as
they are. Your hat

you'll also be needing, that temple
of higher thought, index of
good government.

How far from where you came
or where we go
together?

'A man's hat,' you said,
'should talk
to his shoes.' Do you believe

there are sufficient days
in a life
for mourning

the loss of a life. The voltage of the handshake
the measure of
the man. Electrical circuitry of

his body. Do you believe
in prayers as an endless
questioning, in burial at sea.

That nothing and everything
matters. And the listening shoes
that will hear

but have none of it. Do you still believe
in the good life, not
as we led it but as it is taken

from us, far beyond
telling or asking, whatever else
the hat has

to say. Do you believe now
as you once did?
Then steady

this wavering hand
and quiet this
disbelief.

Asthmatic

A word that came between
sloe and snow –
slow, maybe,
or slower. All that remains

of winter – a gin bottle in
a blackthorn hedge,
penultimate clue
of the 3am crossword – that winter

I forgot to breathe. Nurses in
the snowy uniforms
of their province, as mobile
and attentive as clouds. Later

that was me, coming back across
the air bridge. All I could think
not to wake them. And down the row
of asthmatic trees

the allergy van.
Not a single breath wasted
before or since. All winter
a musical note ascribed

to my breathing, a whitish noise –
sandpaper constellations
rasping the ceiling,
the endless night sky of each

lung, this broad land crossed
in one laboured breath
to lie, Mother, forever in your keeping,
in this, your trembling bed.

Two burning cars, one afternoon

Balclutha fire crews were called out to two vehicle fires in quick succession yesterday afternoon . . . . Both fires were extinguished without injury or further incident. Balclutha fire station officer Stacey Verheul said although it was unusual to have two such incidents on the same day, engine fires were more prevalent in spring . . . . 'Vehicles that haven't been used for a while can quickly become a home for nesting birds . . .' — OTAGO DAILY TIMES, *18 OCTOBER 2018*

Nature is as
nature does, the fire chief
explains. A car is nothing but

an aviary
and all roadworthiness
ends in ruin –

whether you are talking
a Mark III Zephyr
or Mercedes Benz – the bird singing

beneath the bonnet
will find them all.
The car runs out

before the road,
the season
before its bird-life.

In almost-Spring
an engine compartment
offers ideal nesting

and nature is always
held accountable
for the shape of things

gone west
or elsewhere
or otherwise

up in smoke, leaving
our combustible selves
staring skywards

unfeathered, undusted,
supposedly 'without injury or
further incident', no mention of

two parents gone
within one season of a year.
No nest, no nothing.

They were cheap and we were poor

So we bought them – a pair of
orange butterflies pinned behind
sky-blue glass. But now you're
leaving they'll be divided

among the eddying towns, familiar
streams. Our goodbyes have taken months
of all descriptions, down-country
bicycles writing obituaries along

the wet roads. Now you're leaving
your lousy mattress and straw hat
for this whirling bird, this
joyous machine, flying over privet

hedges, your children below waving
goodbye, their hands in their mouths.

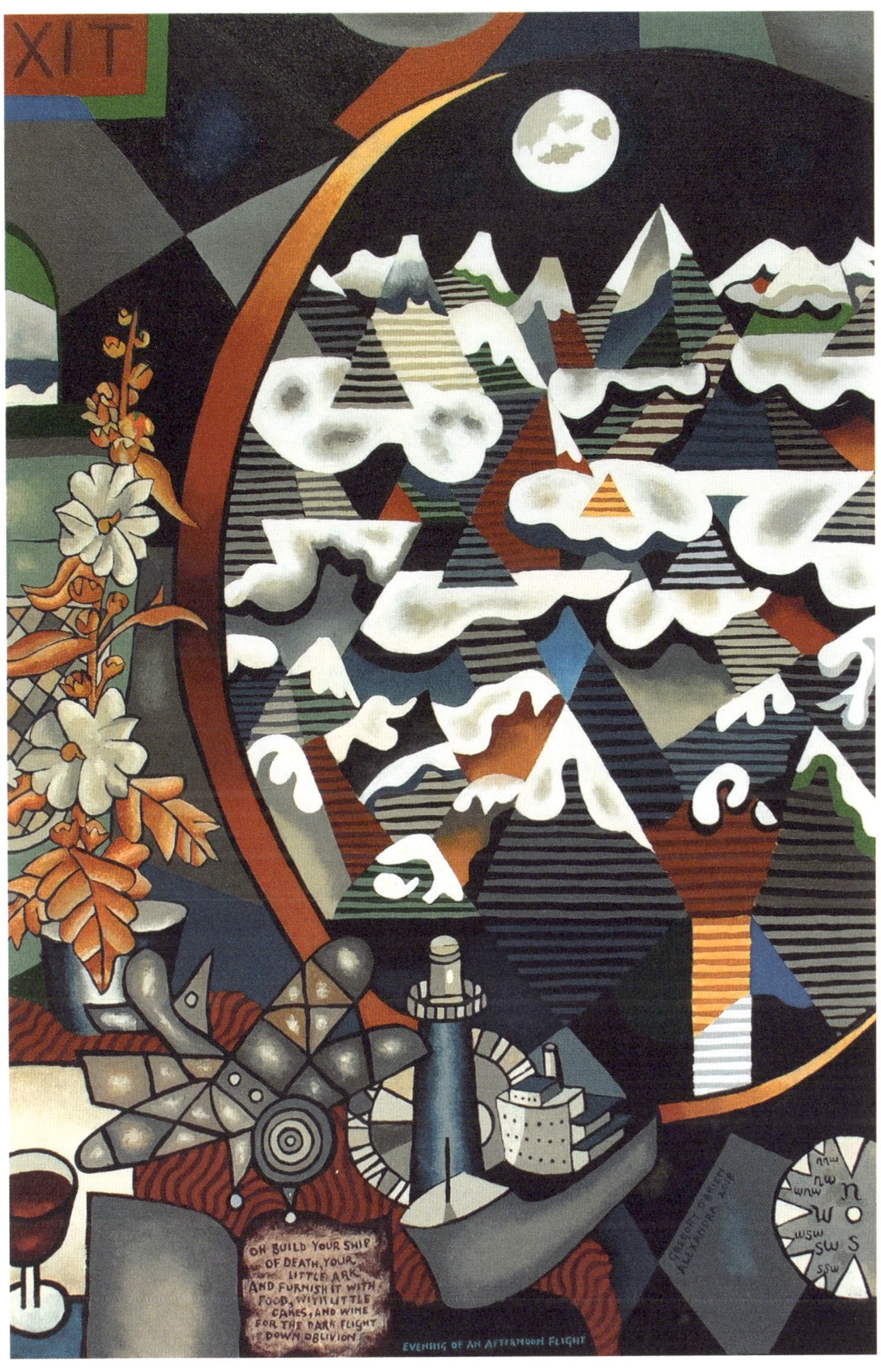
XIT
OH BUILD YOUR SHIP
OF DEATH, YOUR
LITTLE ARK
AND FURNISH IT WITH
FOOD, WITH LITTLE
CAKES, AND WINE
FOR THE DARK FLIGHT
DOWN OBLIVION
EVENING OF AN AFTERNOON FLIGHT
GREGORY O'BRIEN
ALEXANDRA 2018
nnw
nw
wnw
n
w
wsw
sw
s
ssw

9.30am Most of the quakes in the hours and days since the 6.6 have been minor and hardly felt. Yet even the subtlest still elicits a response from our home. A sound like a plucked violin. A plink or a twang. With its utterances and sighs, our dwelling – a double-brick structure, one of eight built in Wellington by a migratory Hungarian, circa 1929 – has come to function as a public address system on behalf of these seismic goings-on, not only announcing them but also interpreting and even commenting upon them. A medium-strength earthquake is, I note, about the same volume as an animal on the roof or under the floor. Weaker quakes elicit a clicking or buzzing – sounds like those of furniture being shifted or a table being set. It is as if a miniature family – a replica of us – is now living in the six-centimetre cavity that exists between the inner and outer walls of our double-brick structure.

The Spaniards of Italian Creek

Speargrass above Lake Dunstan, Central Otago

Urchins of this raised
undersea, at once
ocean-bedded and blue sky'd,

your foreign accent
we forgive you,
your barbed inflorescence

upon which our wits too
are sharpened. In this
the gleaming hour or

golden age of
such things, the water race
that runneth under

low land and lupin, spear-
grass and shotgun shell,
chattering, as if to say

we were expecting you
mid-morning, clad in
edelweiss, spinescent.

Bluebells and coral
lichen make up your bed,
the coolest of linens upon which

this armada sails, these
syllables worn and pressed,
sea eggs of the stratosphere
    in snow's pocket.

Streets and mountains

As the cloud reads the orchard, a swimmer reads the curve of the bay,
an ice-skater reads the surface of the half-frozen lake and, in season,
a fisherman reads the pattern of sea birds. As a chair reads its position at
the table, an aeroplane reads the evening sky and finds a way through.
The weather reads the furrowed brow of the forecaster and is itself,
in turn, read. As ever, a bird reads the absence of birds above a certain
field, just as the streets read the mountains, the mountains the streets,
and have as much to say, as much to say.

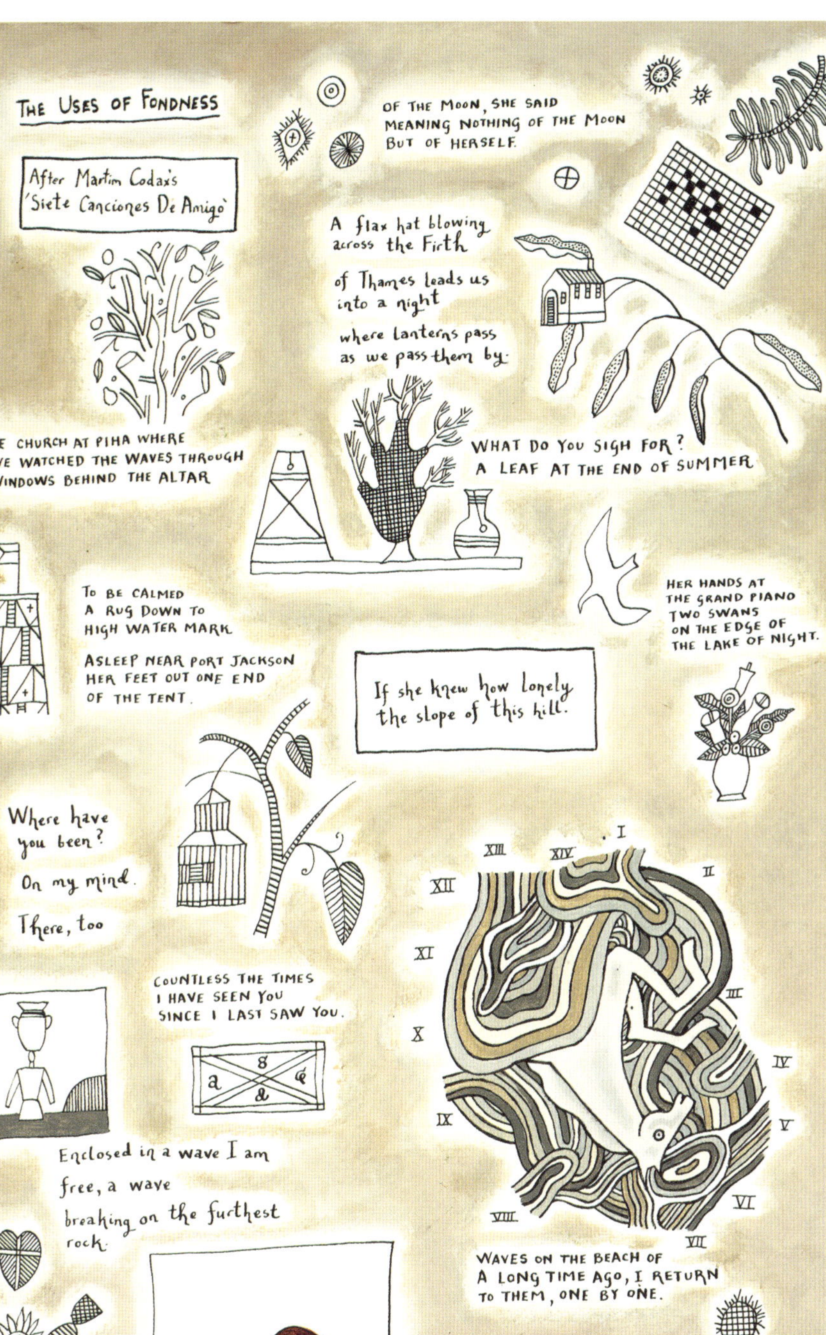
THE USES OF FONDNESS
After Martin Codax's 'Siete Canciones De Amigo'
OF THE MOON, SHE SAID
MEANING NOTHING OF THE MOON
BUT OF HERSELF.
A flax hat blowing across the Firth
of Thames leads us into a night
where lanterns pass as we pass them by.
THE CHURCH AT PIHA WHERE
WE WATCHED THE WAVES THROUGH
WINDOWS BEHIND THE ALTAR
WHAT DO YOU SIGH FOR?
A LEAF AT THE END OF SUMMER
TO BE CALMED
A RUG DOWN TO
HIGH WATER MARK
ASLEEP NEAR PORT JACKSON
HER FEET OUT ONE END
OF THE TENT.
HER HANDS AT
THE GRAND PIANO
TWO SWANS
ON THE EDGE OF
THE LAKE OF NIGHT.
If she knew how lonely
the slope of this hill.
Where have
you been?
On my mind.
There, too
COUNTLESS THE TIMES
I HAVE SEEN YOU
SINCE I LAST SAW YOU.
Enclosed in a wave I am
free, a wave
breaking on the furthest
rock.
WAVES ON THE BEACH OF
A LONG TIME AGO, I RETURN
TO THEM, ONE BY ONE.
Gregory O'Brien
POEM AFTER MARTIN CODAX, MARCH 1987
DRAWN IN APRIL 2017

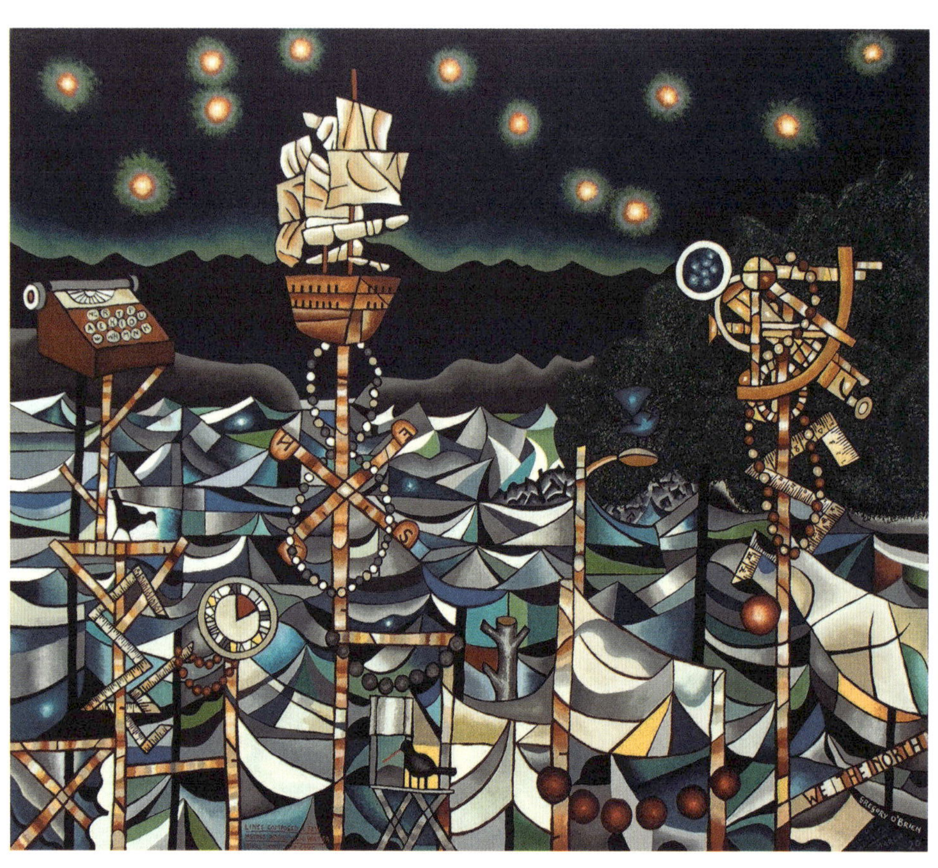
WE THE NORTH
GREGORY O'BRIEN

For James Cook, melancholy, at Meretoto / Ship Cove

An outdoor shower, I would suggest,
if Cook were still here

or at least the ship-worn memory
of a wife

pale as this morning's sea-
fog, clad only

in bafflement, scent of ambergris –
plain to see, or be left

unseen. This life too long for the being
together, too short for such parting.

The Science Tent pitched at Meretoto, 1777

Abide with me, bird-
        feathered dawn
                in the bluster and blur
        of one rediscovered

morning, a rectangle of mainsail
        in the rethinking, a lick
                of dyed fabric, whence
        the nocturnal snoozing
        of specimen boxes, faded colours
    of botanical watercolour
and naval ensign.

Night fires, scurvy grass, a pencil
        outlines the amorous lizard,
                cryptic grasshopper.
        Two hundred years hence, a tee shirt
swims ashore from the cruise ship
        Le Lapérouse, in a spume
                of capitals – WE THE NORTH.
        A monument shaped like a metronome
                marks our place in the music.

Great age of machines

We awoke to the great age of machines. A Valparaíso family gone diagonally up a cliff-face. The winches and exploding harpoons of Quintay. It was 1933, according to the mechanical bellhop recently installed in a hat shop window – reputedly the first robot to reach South America, its cane tapping time on the windowpane.

The age of transistor radios was replaced by the age of things the transistor radio said, and then by the age of only those things that we wanted to hear. It was then we resumed the search for the great age of machines: hands in search of handles in search of doors in search of closets in search of rooms in search of houses in search of suburbs . . .

Later, we ducked down an alley to avoid the great age of machines: police vans with marauding water cannons – a sprinkler system tending the hatless and the helmeted, both sides jostling for the future.

A girl threw a rock, a boy a flower. Two policewomen slept together in a park. Small rooms on wires went careering up the harbour-front hills; machines adjusted the tension of the miscellaneous stringed instruments of Providencia. Things were said. A woman's lips were a red bird reflected in a visor.

Then we said goodbye to the great age of machines. We adjusted the brightness. Goodbye also to the exhausted Coquito palm, victim of its own sugary sap, the last forest swallowed up by the last wine cask. These final years, days, minutes and seconds of the age of machines overtaken by a wave of dogs, bicycles and women on dizzying heels, looking down on this world laid out beneath them.

Three postcards from Valparaíso

I

The staircase and then
the ladder, the ladder
and then the funicular, the alley
and then the steps, the staircase
up to the Pelican & Vulture
the staircase up to the colour blue
the staircase up to the songs of Violeta Parra
the staircase up to the number 86
the staircase up to the multitudinous skies
of Chile, the staircase up to the calcium deposits of
distant stars as seen through telescope or
upraised wine bottle, the staircase up
to the odes of Pablo Neruda
and the staircase back down.

II *Graffiti and 'the future of good government'*

Rising tide
of green and pink spray-paint

advancing, with stealth
on the hilltop barracks.

III

Upwardly mobile citizens
of Valparaíso:
      Mister Colorista on his

paint-spattered ladder, Mister
Primitivista in his
            skyward hat box, his

private funicular. And
Mister Tribalista's
praiseworthy odes

to the flaming tree
the back half of a dog
the goddess of cats.

9.50am 'What happens to us / Is irrelevant to the world's geology / But what happens to the world's geology / Is not irrelevant to us.' It was Alan Riach who pointed me to Hugh MacDiarmid's 'On a Raised Beach' with its sobering but also steadying thought for these unsteadying times. Another 'strong' quake has just rolled through. A 4.9. Maybe 20 seconds in duration. This force which keeps pushing things towards us as well as away from us, and which keeps dropping things – what is it trying to say to us?

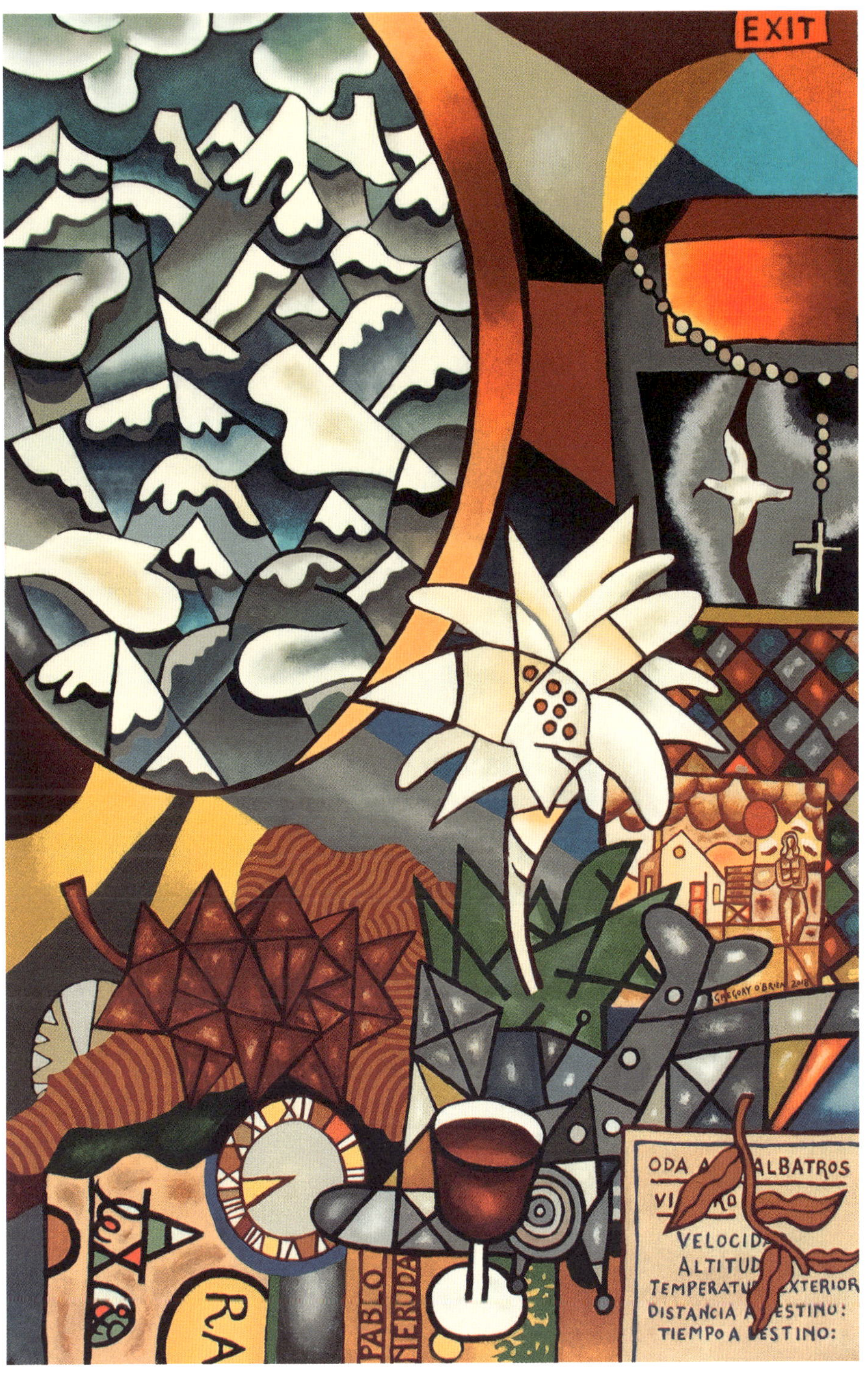
EXIT
GREGORY O'BRIEN 2018
PABLO NERUDA
RA
ODA A ALBATROS
VI RO
VELOCIDA
ALTITUD
TEMPERATU EXTERIOR
DISTANCIA A ESTINO:
TIEMPO A ESTINO:

Styx Crossing, Upper Taieri

Gone without weskit and wilderberry,
crystal apple and the hat rack

in the sky, empty of what we were.
Gone shoeless, bare-legged

into the netherworld, with neither
forwarding address nor date

of return, emptied of what
we were. With neither boatman

nor Mrs Grace's punt, gone without
waders and burlap and 'Home James and

don't spare the horses', you were frozen-footed
carrying a blind dog across

the Styx, while I searched for my name
among those
    carved into the strongroom ceiling

from JOLLY & JOLLY, DUNEDIN to
CAROL-JOY HISLOP SADLY DEPARTING

THIS LAND 26.5.68, all of them
gone beyond mountain mangle and all-seeing eye,

gone without so much as
a weather-beaten dog, mid-river, blind, carried.

for Grahame and Milo

Styx, Central Otago, late summer

As it happens
over fellfield and peneplain,
            as if
      raining. On weedle and wedge
and Mr Haye's lone metal arm,

                  as if snowing.

Over blue tussock and somnambulant
lawn,
                  the sun gone
lightly
      from bough to bulb and
everything between,

      a cricket ball bowled

not particularly well
at nothing
      in particular.

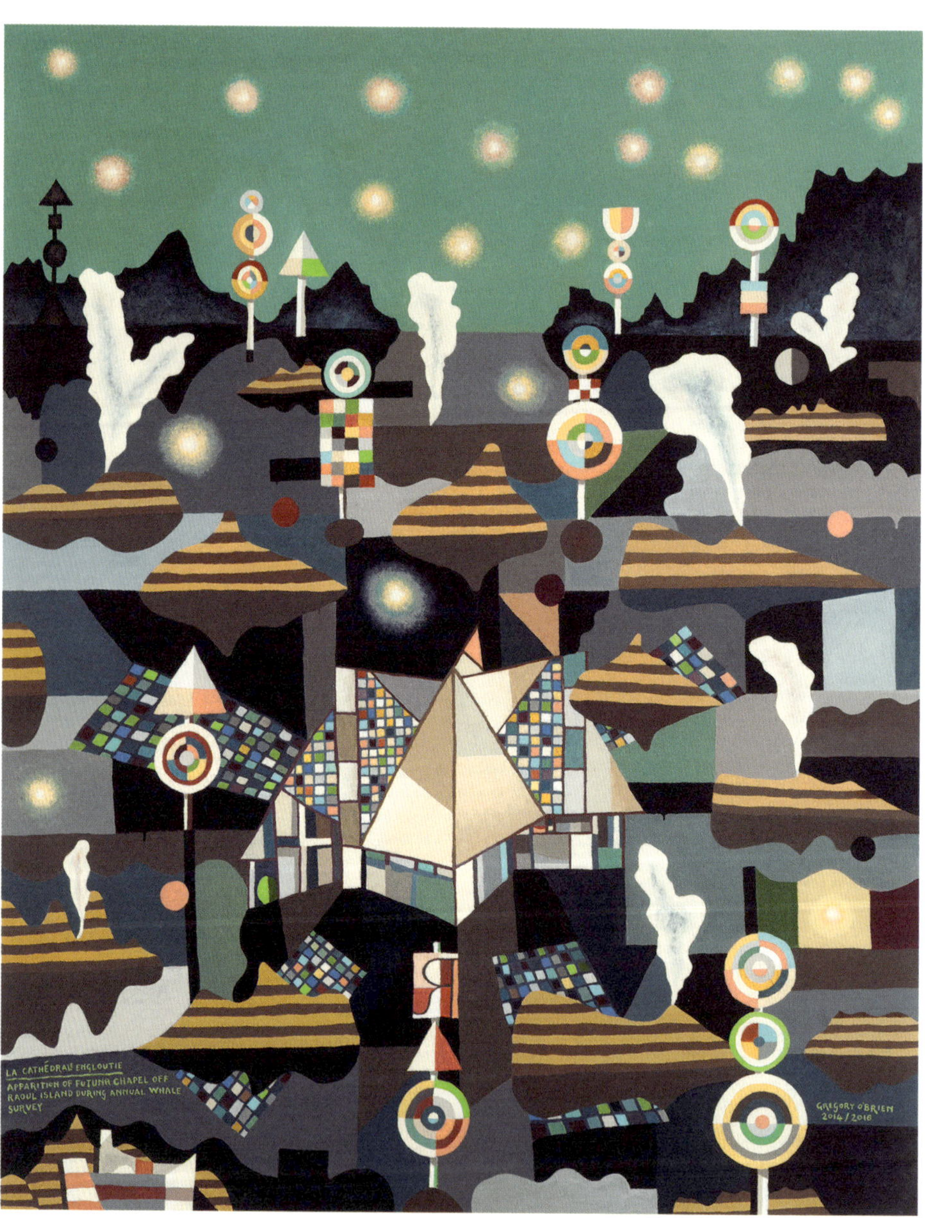
LA CATHÉDRALE ENGLOUTIE
APPARITION OF FUTUNA CHAPEL OFF RAOUL ISLAND DURING ANNUAL WHALE SURVEY
GREGORY O'BRIEN
2014 / 2016

A genealogy

We are injured; we hurt
easily – our genes
          decided that

for us – as my mother decided
early on, I would have an occupation

beginning with the letter p, coming
as I was
          as we all were

from a line of policemen, publicans
and pig-farmers: three p's
          loudly stated

unlike those three adjacent p's
found lately on a musical
          score – *pianississimo.*

Hence, but less than
intentionally
          I became a poet

a slight variation upon
the typewriter keys, my genes
          a further

variation, played and occasionally
listened to –
          like the violinist

on St Patrick's Bridge, adjusting the angle
of her instrument so it doesn't
          fill with rain.

‡

Here in the Petri dish
of the page or
          rain-dampened field

we address these like-minded
cells, familiar genes
          in ribbons and chains

knotted and spliced and set
afloat in the broad pool
          of all the people
                    we might have been.

‡

The studious genes we were told about
but somehow lacked;
        an ungainliness

of the fingers, however, we blamed upon
the familial pool – generations of us
        unable to bend

the accordion. Yet we did know
or our genes told us
        how music might agitate

or unravel the minutiae of us:
genes, cells, chromosomes, DNA
        rattling like heirlooms on an unstable

mantelpiece. Whatever else we had
to blame or thank them for:
        an inability to juggle, swim,

to keep a straight face, our
appalling timing and
        ramshackle emotions, how it was

we sought the company
of bullish men and
        swanlike women.

‡

A day's sailing out on the broad pond
of the self – this was where
    we finally caught up

with ourselves, reflected in the
shallow-ended pool, and in the pattern
    of hail falling

on Pope's Quay, or in the molecular
structure of a room filled
    with musicians – the accordion

not so much as it breathed
for us or with us
    but as it moved

the air and its contents along
in spite of us, and the violin played
    as though it was being

wrestled down from
a top shelf or attic, wrenched

from the deathly blackness
that will silence
    us all.

‡

This pond, this flood, this
sufficiency – how it is
          we ascribe singularity

to such a multitude. And the migratory drift
of a roomful of chairs
          musicwards; the long necks and birds' heads

of violins dipping into
a salmon-rich sea. But where
          discreetly to place

the music stands
mid-stream or mid-tune? And where in the wider
          scheme of things – human history being

yet another branch or offshoot of genetics
endlessly elaborating
          upon itself – so runs

one stream of thought, the other
a bridge high above it
          and upon which

coins dance
in an upturned hat.

‡

We are numb to them –
the promptings
          of the heart and the rain-patter

of coins, generous souls; the moonlit
pond or raging sea on which
          our genes make their way

alone or in formation, in less than
favourable conditions, another kind of
          genetic storm, a welter or tumult

in which fishes and the odd
rowing skiff
          are caught up

and rolled over
and occasionally
          have their say.

‡

The blood's velocity through
the veins
          precisely that

of the tidal waters under Christy Ring Bridge
where floats the origami swan
          and *Irish Examiner*

the ear trained on
the passing of such things:
          the crooked mile

the unstraight face
if ever there was
          such a place.

for the two other Gregorys, Delanty and Orr
Cork, February 2012

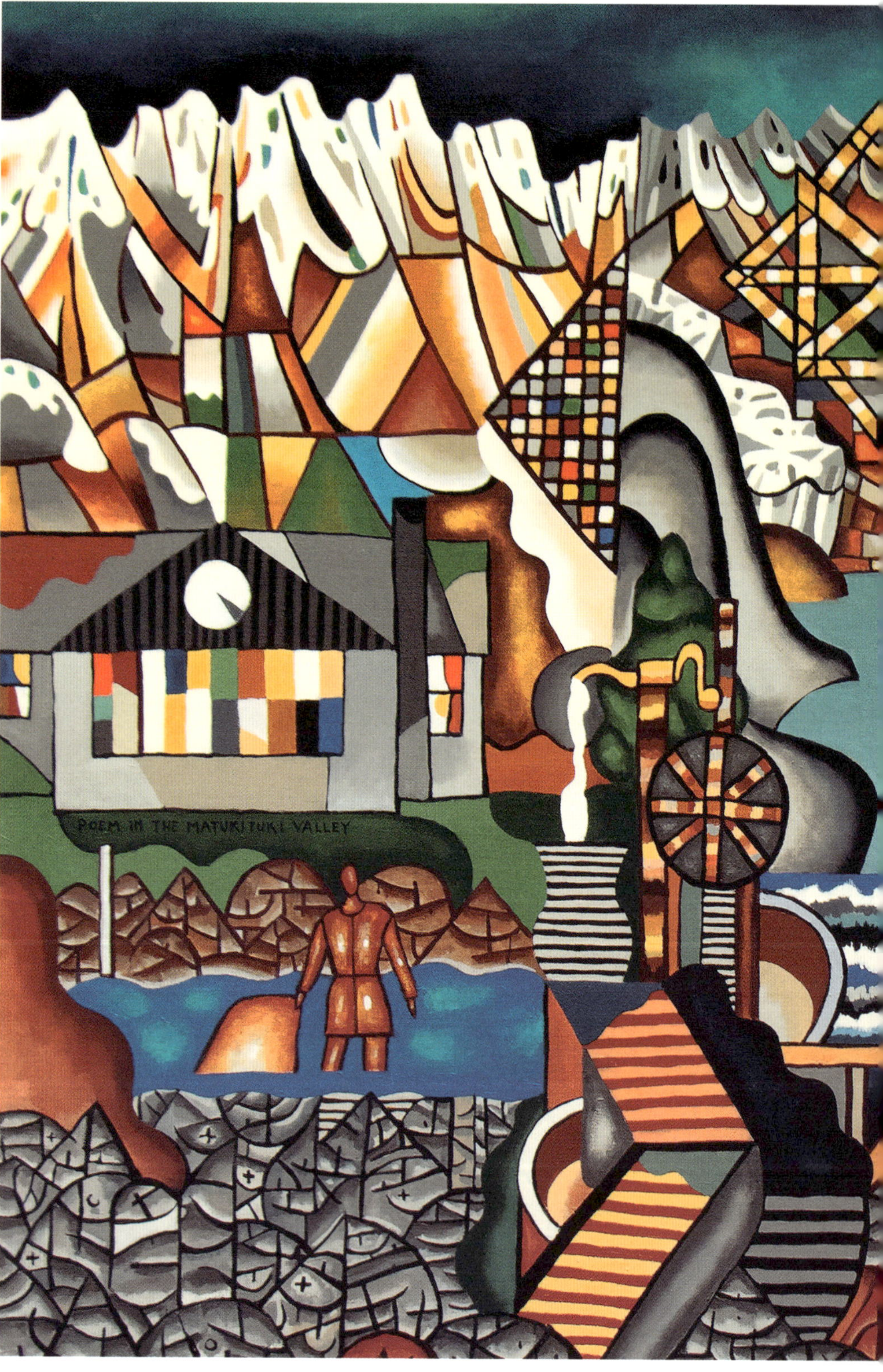
POEM IN THE MATUKITUKI VALLEY

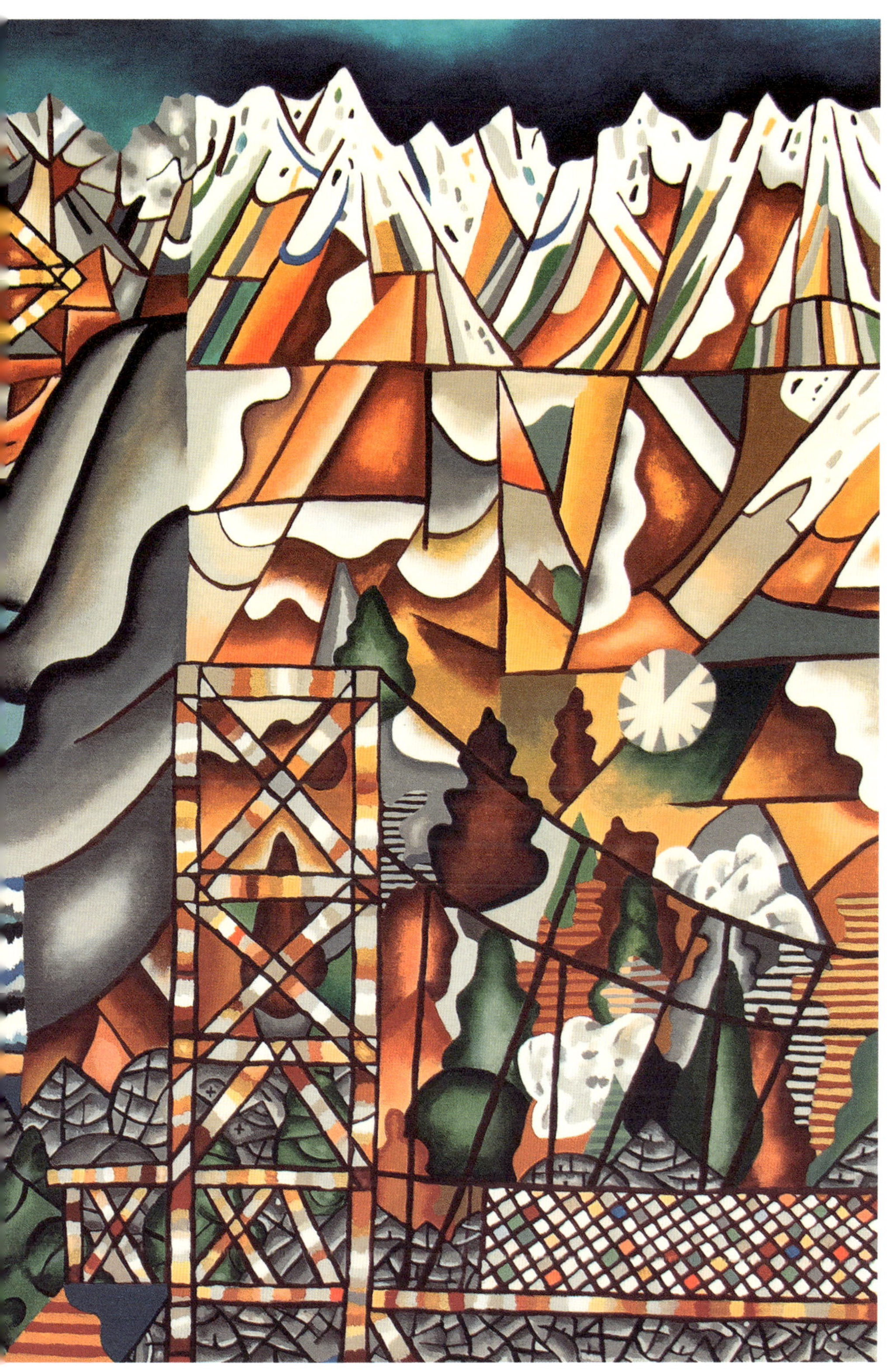

A device for bird-catching, The Snares and Rakiura

Boarded and hammered
mileage of the long walk eastwards,
Mason Bay to Freshwater –

hardly a stitch-
bird or a song the entire way, only
a pair of women's stockings

strung between trackside
matagouri. For the sake of
science, a fernbird

lured by its own
pre-recorded tune,
flight interrupted

by Virginia's repurposed
leggings, from which
she will unwind

her crash-landed pilot
for a pinprick of blood,
tweaked from that place

where underwing
meets gently feathered
fuselage. Sized and surveyed, beak

to tail, wing to wing-
tip, her droplet
of song is released back into

that freewheeling space
so freshly measured
in lengths

of a woman's stockinged
leg. Also turning homewards,
Virginia and her

wingman, test tube
in rucksack, icepack
and box of birdsong,

their researches ever-advancing,
ornithology aside,
into the lesser properties

of stockings
struck on a northerly axis,
ensnaring.

11.28am And now the house is vibrating again . . . a 'moderate' three-point-something, trailing off. It makes me think of a cat's purring, or the hum and vibration of a rowing skiff when it reaches a certain speed. Or an acoustic effect. A variation upon J. S. Bach. A well-tempered something.

The library ladder

Always or most often, five steps up
or four back down, a right turn

and a yachtsman's reach, orchestral
conduction or tennis serve,

an unexpected title or simply
endless blue sky

at each fingertip. Three rungs down
the fictional steps, a librarian

like a book, might be unshelved or, stepping
from cloud to cloud, dust-

jacketed, descend the lighthouse stairs
of everything ever

written about or wanting
to be. Another adjustment of

the well-versed steps, the vertical alphabet
advances further skyward,

with its marginalia of birds, flyleaves, all that is
cut and unbound. Two steps back

to ground level and she finds herself
between wetland clearance

and plausible farming – ever mindful,
in these well-tended aisles that

an insecure shelf can become
a downpour, the library floor

a floodplain, replete with trout hatchery,
jockey club and this, the adjacent orchard

where a woman, long of limb,
finds herself halfway

down or up a ladder, flax basket
laden with persimmons,

apples or it doesn't matter
what – the yet to be

written about fruit,
the waiting world.

for Lydia Wevers

Signing

It comes back to you. At the School
for the Deaf, the waltzing class,
a balloon placed between each couple

to maintain appropriate
distance. 'You were that much taller
and then some.' This afternoon's

balloon replaced with a flutter
of hands, as if gathering altitude, as if
'I could fall from

the height of you.' It comes back
as a vocabulary or untethering,
for every outward breath, a breath

breathed in. The space between us that once
might have whispered 'I am listening' or
'I can see you
through the red balloon.'

12 noon The most unlikely things have been rendered articulate. *They have not voices, yet they sing . . .* We find ourselves listening attentively to objects that we didn't realise have sounds. We listen to the music of toothbrushes jostling in a mug on the bathroom window ledge; we recognise the sound a guitar tuner makes as it advances along a wooden shelf, the metallic rattle of cutlery in a drawer, ceramic sounds of crockery, and the frames of paintings bumping against walls as if they wanted to be let in. We are learning other things as well: that hardback books travel further than paperbacks (they absorb shock less effectively – that's as far as my deliberations have progressed). Tall vases move further and at greater speed than short ones; they also fall over sooner, and break more easily. The hidden identities of things have also been revealed. The cordless phone, like a diver on a high board, leaps gracefully from its base and explodes on the floor.

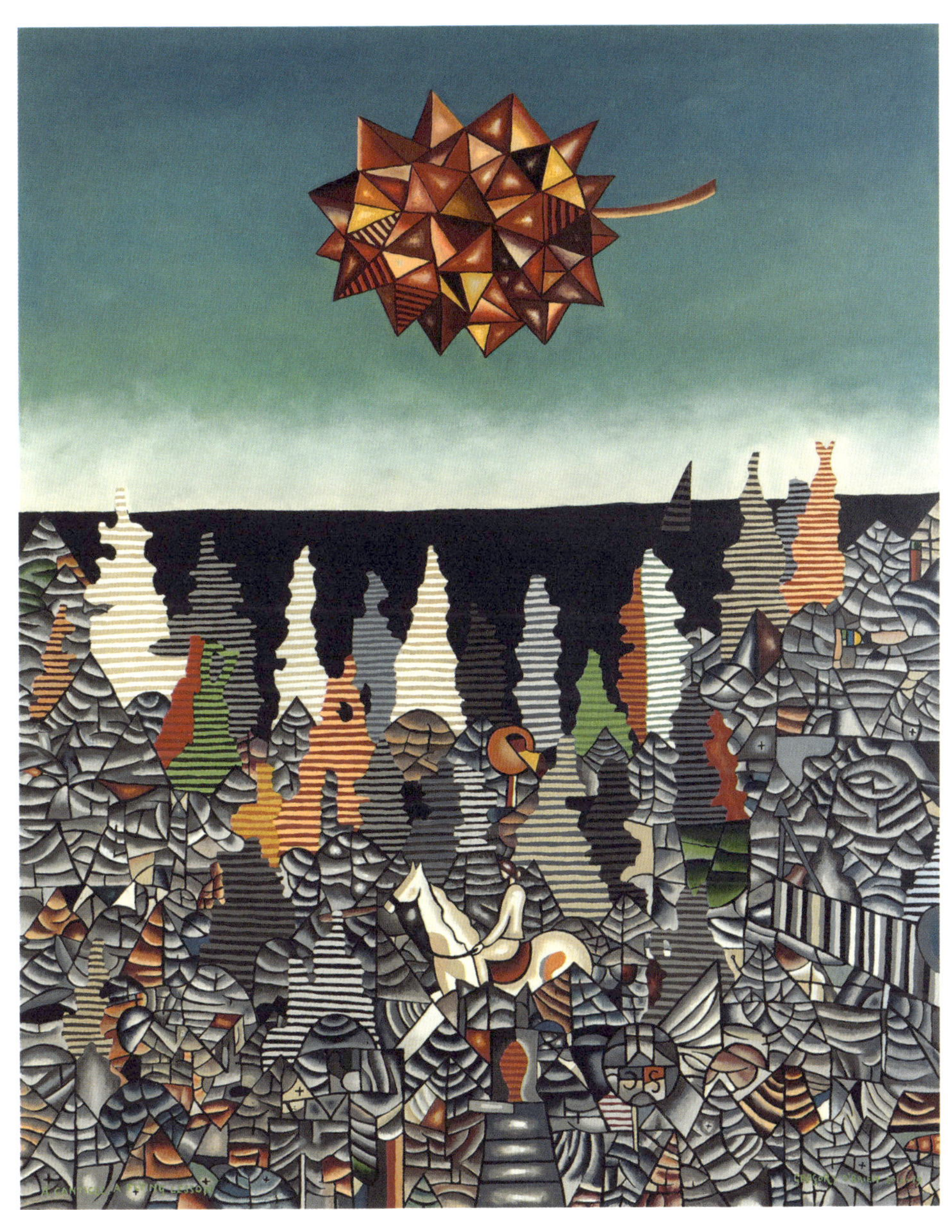

Song of the coral brain

And this was the day
the lord made
the scuttling crab

and this was
the day the choir sang
their song hammered into

these Latin roads.
And this is the day worn
as sea egg or coral star

a green headdress or
land crab boiling on the rim
of a car wheel

the white coral church
weighing anchor.

for John Pule
Liku, Niue

Ōpunake, Taranaki

I have no breath but yours, nor
as many words – the orchard

a tumble of fruit; the mountain again
in its lather of cloud.

Surf cast or reeled in, the sun
in a whitebait net, or waylaid

mid-afternoon, between *Everybody's*
and *The Enterprise*. And the mountain always

on your shoulder. A Torana gone
around the clock, near-new moon

on its bonnet. Long line
and lure, beach break and

unquilted mountain,
wayward one.

for Stephen Hickey

Conversation with a mid-Canterbury braided river

Fifteen apparitions have I seen;
The worst a coat upon a coat-hanger.
(W. B. Yeats, 'The Apparitions')

Moved, as I am
immovable, like you

I turn over, I sleep
on my side

nestled in the
watery fact

of you. I fall about, collect
my thoughts –

another thing we have
in common – I get ahead

of myself, I meander
so as not to

lose my way. I rock
and sway.

I digress. And this is how
I come back to you

bedded and besotted, body strewn
with inverted clouds

migratory birds, dawn-lit
improbable.

Like you, I have
my sources; I wade

the long waters
of myself. My ear

to the ground or
the constant applause

of your rapids. You are your own
concert, open-air, a solitary leaf

crowd-surfing downstream
and the occasional

beer can thrown. Lately there has been
talk of you as

lapsed or recovering, dispersed
drained, interrupted or

resumed. And this
my sleepless night, my apparition:

an insect walking this land –
a coat-hanger on which might

hang a bright green shirt, a stream led down
a long avenue of hosepipe and

aluminium, a river flowing
sideways, its taniwha

reduced to a drizzle or fine mist
a trickle from

an automated tap. Your position on this too
is inarguable

as if argument was ever
a river's way.

Braided, you tell me, I was
upbraided, scrambled across

siphoned and run ragged by hydro trader, flood
harvester, water bottler, irrigator

and resource manager. This riverbed is
my marae, the long legs of wading birds

my acupuncture, these waters
my only therapy.

On clear nights
galaxies enter me, planetary bodies

like swimmers. How many minds
a river has – caddis and mayfly

eyeless eel and
native trout. As an argument

this might not hold water
but neither does

a paddock gone around
in circles

or a skeletal arm endlessly
scrawling its initials in

a sodden green ledger. Whichever way
the river doesn't flow

I remain undecided, as is
water's way.

I disperse, lost for words
I dry up.

I saw an apparition, an insect
walking this riverless land

earthbound stars
rattling, beyond reflection

along a dry
river's bed.

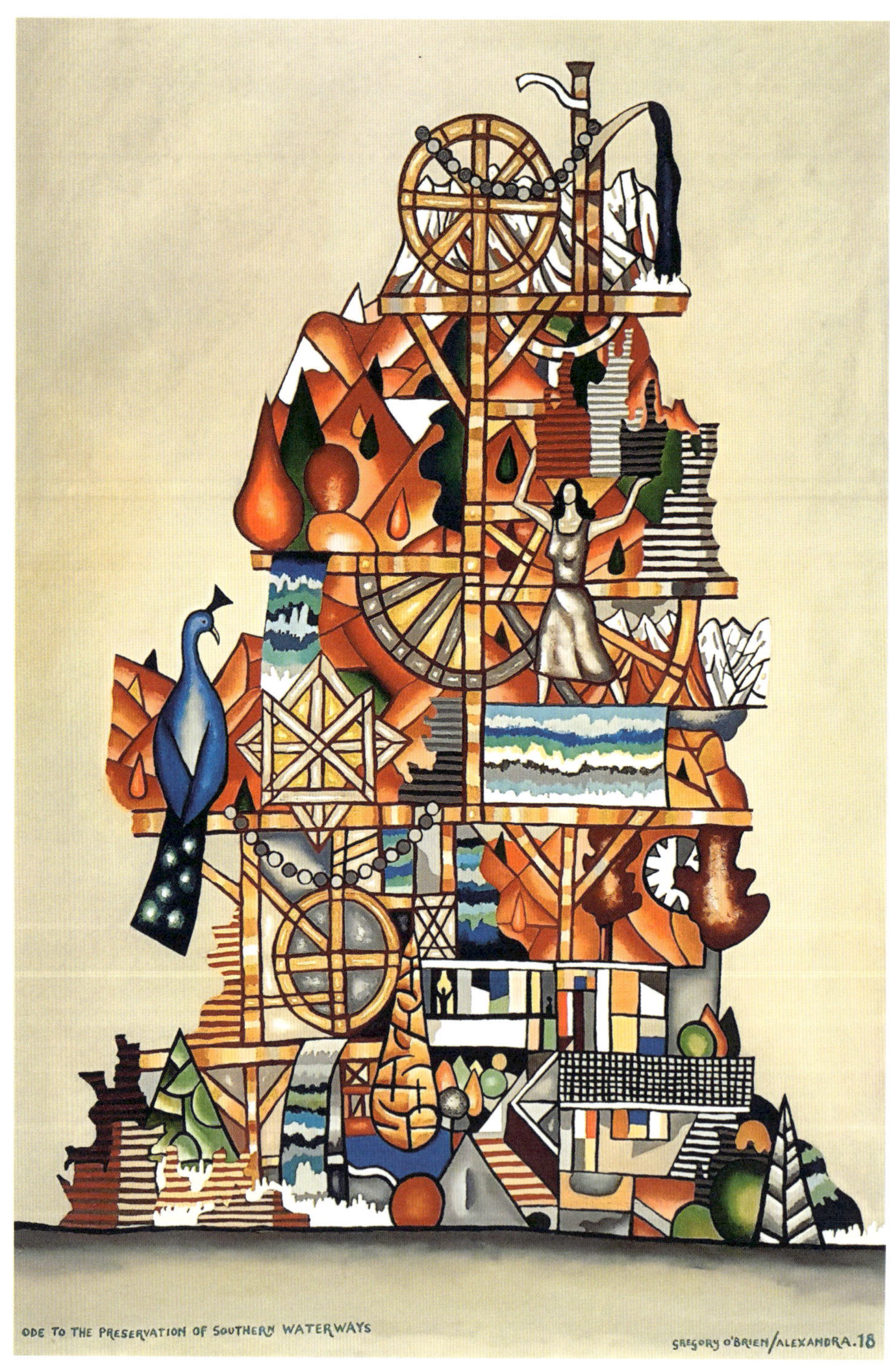
ODE TO THE PRESERVATION OF SOUTHERN WATERWAYS
GREGORY O'BRIEN/ALEXANDRA.18

Sixteen things

Rundle St

Two-dollar sunglasses
Seven-dollar shoes
Six-dollar souvenir

'the girl you keep in your head or
the girl you keep in your life'

Five-dollar cover charge
Threepenny Opera
Thirty-dollar bike

‡

P. M. (Afternoon of a painter)

Piet Mondrian

Pet Monster

‡

Orchestra

who is
playing
what

‡

i.m. John Ashbery

A bird gone
missing
from its feathers

this way
you went
from us.

‡

For the Jodhpur Maharajas

anything with a bell attached

anything with a chapel built upon it

anything which is periodically covered by an ocean

anything dressed as a woman
    that is not a woman

anything with a flock of migrating birds directly above

anything with accompanying musical merriment

anything that finds itself unwittingly adorned with
    peacock feathers

anything with a moustache that is also a fish

anything upon which the ground-plan of a city
    might be based

‡

Squirrel's requiem for Sun Ra, Central Park

Evening divided
among the brass section

each note
a far planet. How, many years earlier

you awoke one morning, a crown
upon your head – a bird's nest or

tangle of snakelike metal –
above a face upon which

rain would always appear to have
just fallen. Now I must replace you

with music
the exact shape of you.

‡

Among bluebells

Among forget-me-nots
Among golden Spaniards
Among snow tussock
Among penwipers
Among scree and snowberry
Among sundew
Willowherb, woollyhead.

‡

M. C.

mister cool

mystical

‡

For Robyn Marsack — In praise of the Scottish Poetry Library

Skittish Pottery, Lombardy

Scattered pewter lionery

Latvian Skeleton Key

Sleeping Boy Scout Jamboree

Slovenian Rock and Rollery

Turkish Lullaby Refinery

Scuttlefish, Butterfly, Floatery

‡

Sea kelp observed at Makara Beach, on the day of Samuel Beckett's death, 22 December 1989

murmurabilia

‡

Orchard and Reserve

I
pōhutukawa
problem child

II
karaka tree
karaoke

III
mandarin
meandering

IV
guava
god save her

for Paula Green

‡

Ode to DNA

You take me out
to this
the only party
in town.

†

Moot and Pixie

an Elizabethan romance

Moot and Pixie, amorous
at Athenree, their names
    inscribed freshly

on trig and gate and upended
dinghy. Moot, recumbent
    commences his breathless

balladry. And the grasses
sang, as grasses can,
    'Nearer, my god, to thee.'

‡

Lyric

This time she had kicked him out for good.
But he was back, his hat on the kitchen tap –
somewhere a motorcycle, somewhere

a ladder. Twenty-three years and childless, she said,
like twenty-three lamp posts leading off into distance,
evenly spaced. His shoes left on her rug.

Insects walked out of them. Whatever it means
it means nothing, she said. But this time
the green cardigan across the armchair

and the neighbour's cat were on her side.
This time she had kicked him out for good.

‡

Beach house

Were the beach
a house, the sea
a wall, the sun

a shower, then
what would we
owe you, how

would we
know you, both as
beach or house

polished moon
crossing a
polished floor?

‡

Lay me down

On a bed of roses
A bed of an ocean
A bed of ringing telephones
A bed of lettuce
A bed of gulls, landing
A bed of ashes
A bed of Wednesdays
A bed of a river
A bed of other half-remembered or long-forgotten beds
A bed of gulls, taking off

for Ken Bolton

1pm Teams of helmeted men and women bearing clipboards have appeared around the city, paying particular attention to concrete walls, lift wells and chimneys. Buildings are being yellow-stickered, red-stickered, made to proclaim their earthquake-proneness. Behavioural patterns are being revised as well. Like petty criminals, people in shops, cinemas or offices are always checking the availability of doorways, hiding places, tables that might be sheltered beneath, or window frames that might be jumped through.

So far this earthquake season, the greater city of Wellington has escaped relatively lightly. The most visible damage has been some cracks in the asphalt and a disappearing chunk of foreshore. With their different rates of sway, two adjoining buildings in Featherston St have bashed the concrete edges off one another. In Willis St, hotel windows have vacated their frames and smashed in the street below. Walking through town yesterday, what I thought was a clinging vine on the concrete wall of an office block turned out to be a network of cracks. From the downtown supermarket last Friday reports came of milk flagons leaping from the shelves like middle-aged men going feet first into a swimming pool. The cleaning products aisle became a swamp of green liquid.

For the most part, luckily, this has been a quaking of smallish things; nature appears to be observing a certain decorum, making this a perplexing rather than a calamitous time. Yet the nervous system remains on high alert; you hear beyond the usual spectrum of sound; things appear in heightened focus and your sense of time, amidst all this rumbling, is stretched and distorted.

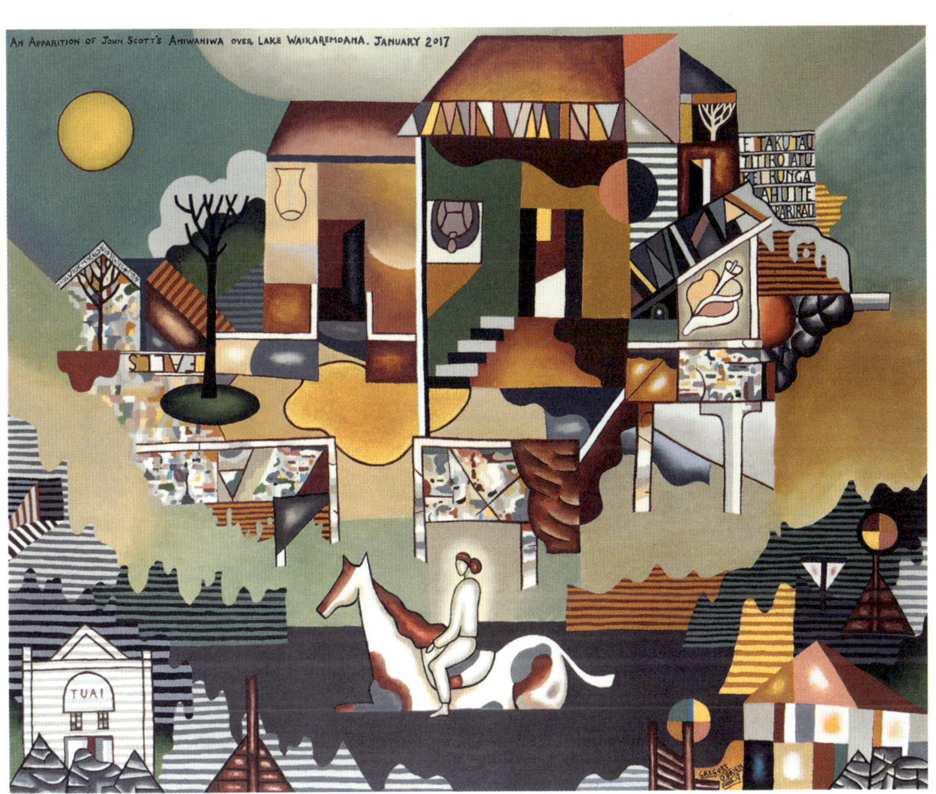
AN APPARITION OF JOHN SCOTT'S ANIWANIWA OVER LAKE WAIKAREMOANA. JANUARY 2017
E TAKU TAU
TITIRO ATU
KEI RUNGA
AHU TE
PARIRAU
TUAI

Lines composed a few metres from Aniwaniwa Visitors Centre on the day of its demolition

The dispossessed stars,
the roof above our heads
trodden underfoot.

For Carlo, a biplane flying low over the Mataura River

Gypsy or Tiger, mothlike
you find your
        wings, or at least
their reflection
mid-river – this bird in which
the two of us
        are nested. Whatever else

has gone, inverted, down-
stream, or been cast
    from this far bridge –
        earrings of
a failed romance, a ukulele
mid-song. Cut of that same cloth

a ream of late afternoon sky
the sunset a parley
    of aeroplane parts, what
you imagined
        I imagined.

Mandeville, October 2018

1.45pm A few weeks back, I was driving through the centre of earthquake-flattened Christchurch. Traffic is still in a perpetual state of re-routing on account of pot-holing, liquefaction and all manner of public works to set these problems right. Bright orange cones – 'witches' hats' – trail across streets, rendering the most simple of car trips circuitous and time-consuming. According to my taxi driver, there were now over three million of these cones in the city. At a cost of $20 each, he told me, they have made someone very, very wealthy. Still, the council has to keep buying more, to compensate for the number crushed beneath service vehicles or stolen by hoodlums. He added that there was one thing about Christchurch you could be certain of: the city would be needing many more of these cones. He then commented, obliquely, that after his death he would like to come back as one of these traffic cones.

A lesser member of the family of Michael Collins, Cork

A marked man
skirting the Roundy
    and Malt Shovel

then crossing an adjacent bridge
which also goes by the name
    Collins. Beneath me, the river which

in this land of related things
must also be
    a not-too-distant cousin

and on each street corner further branches
of the family – bankers, impresarios
    of the Last Great Boom –

their faces I recognise as barnacles
on the hull of the *Julia*, her ladyship
    yet another

cousin you might have loved
for her American accent,
fallible tone – a camera-wary Roberts

or just another Collins – a salt spray
or industrious crew to scrub
    the flank of her

at the tail end
of this large, undulating
    weekend, the extended

or over-extended
family following dutifully
    the bowling match

to the grinding accompaniment
of 'Half Man Half Bicycle'
      at Mannix and Culhane.

Paula Rego

A song

Each her own
orchestra, cathedral
or dance hall, all of us
wild, untimely girls

in the grasp of the room, each body
unaccustomed to itself – she of
the fiery head, the unconventional
menagerie, this the ticket

and over there
the window, and
here upon us
that window's light.

A charm

Each to her own
and to

each other
another.

2.30pm It is now two months since I visited Santiago de Chile. I was installing an exhibition in the Museo de Arte Contemporáneo, working alongside architect / designer Cristian Valdes. Having clambered up a scaffold, Cristian and I were peering down into the cavity within a three-metre-high wall which he had designed especially for the exhibition. While we were doing this, a team of 'maestros' was putting the finishing touches to the second of these two freestanding walls – gib-board structures laid over steel skeletons. Cristian explained to me that these walls were based upon a prototype he had been devising as a new kind of house-design: a 'summer house' which could open outwards from its single, metre-deep wall. Off-season, the dwelling would pack away – collapsing in on itself like an old-fashioned camera with bellows. The summer-lives of the residents could also, accordingly, be stowed or folded away, and remain that way until the next season. He also proffered another potential usage: these inhabitable walls could be shipped around the country, stacked on the back of trucks like books on a shelf, to be used as a highly mobile form of emergency housing.

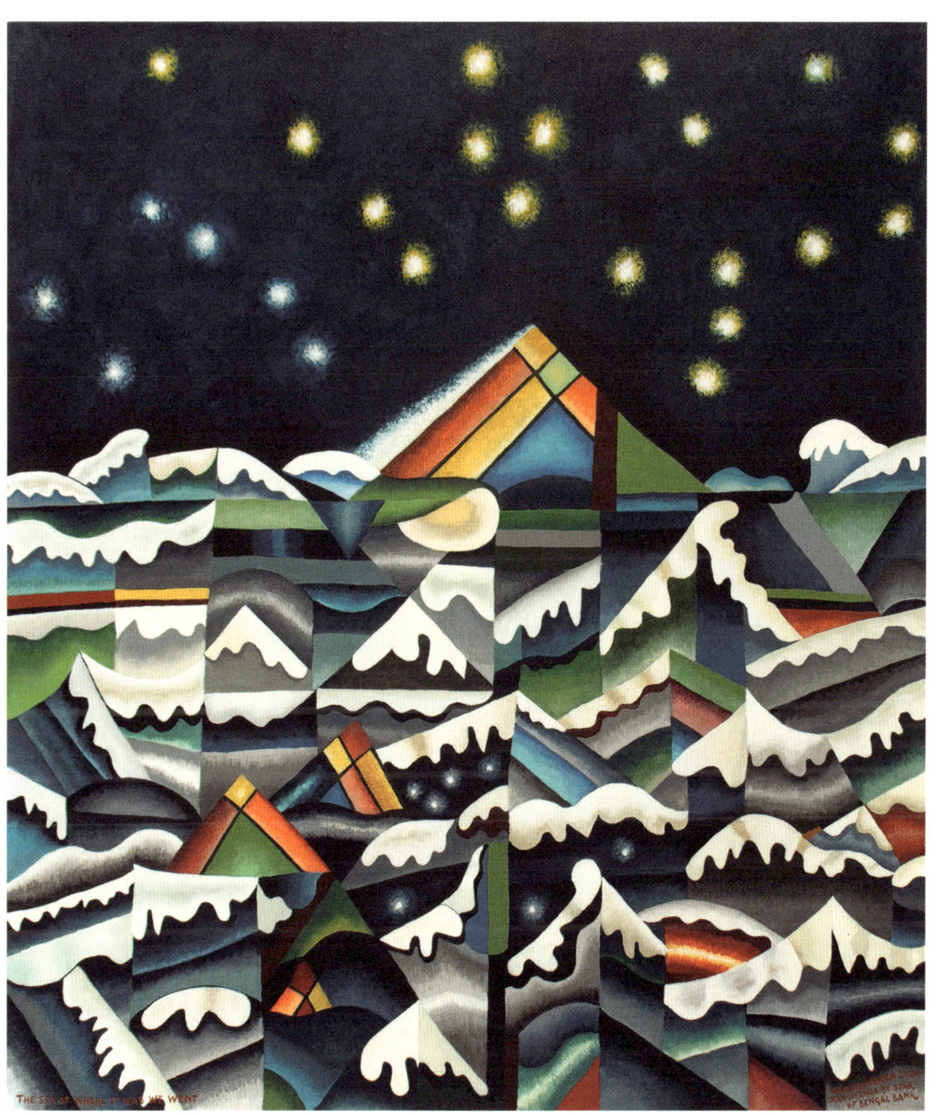
THE SEA OF WHERE IT WAS WE WENT
OF BENGAL BANK

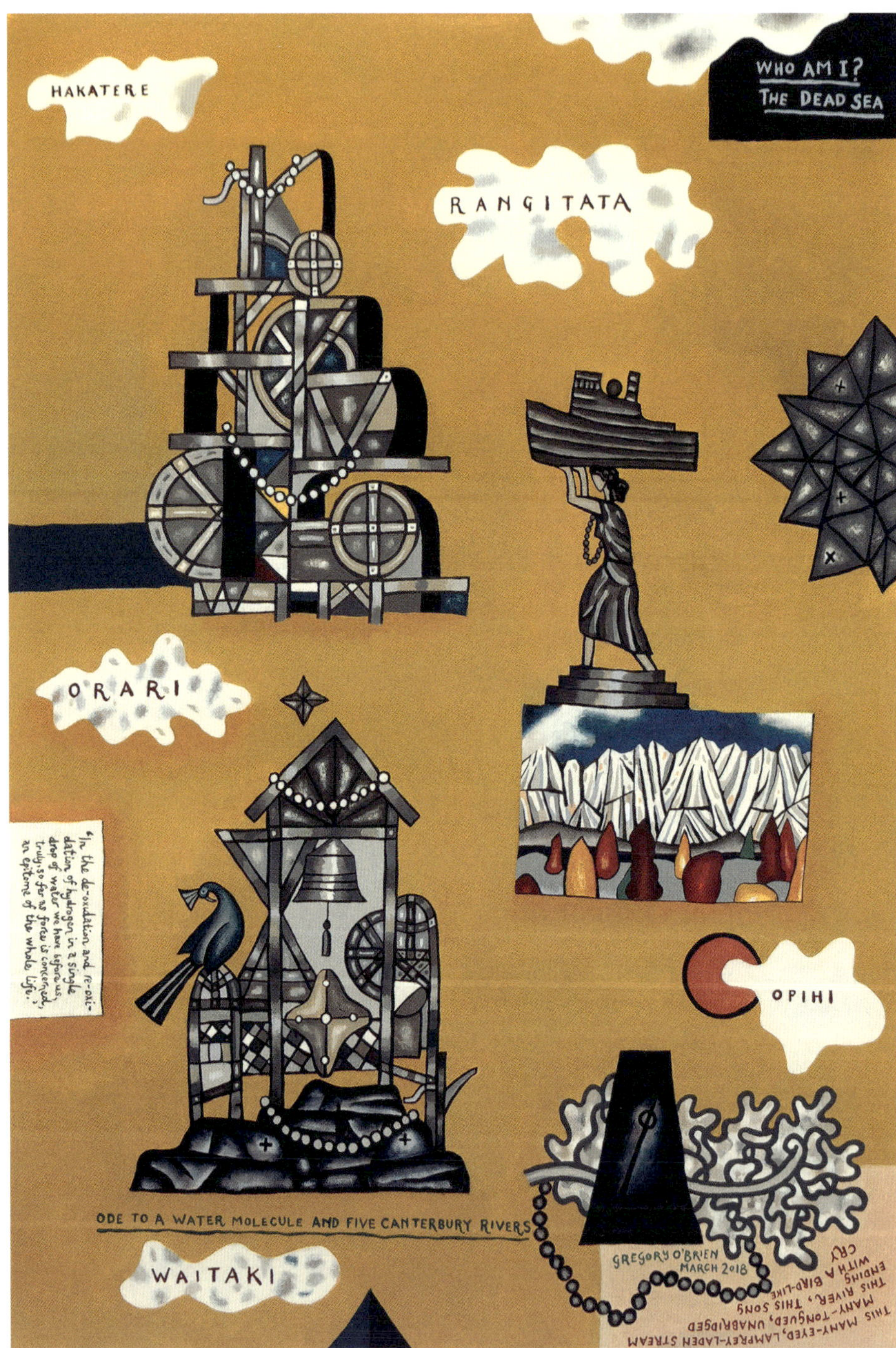

WHO AM I?
THE DEAD SEA
HAKATERE
RANGITATA
ORARI
'In the de-oxidation and re-oxidation of hydrogen in a single drop of water we have before us, truly, so far as force is concerned, an epitome of the whole life.'
OPIHI
ODE TO A WATER MOLECULE AND FIVE CANTERBURY RIVERS
WAITAKI
GREGORY O'BRIEN
MARCH 2018
THIS MANY-EYED, LAMPREY-LADEN STREAM
THIS MANY-TONGUED, UNABRIDGED
THIS RIVER, THIS SONG
ENDING
WITH A BIRD-LIKE
CRY

Ode to the water molecule

Promiscuous, by some accounts,
or simply playing the field –
    indecisive, yet so decidedly
yourself, you are

all these things: ice flow,
cloud cover,
    bend of a river,
crystalline structure

on an aeroplane window, fire-
bucket or drop
in the ocean, dissolver of a morning's
    tablets or

mountain range. We envy you
your irresolution,
        the way you get along
with yourself, as glacier
    or humidity of

an overheated afternoon. A glass
of pitch-black water
            drunk at night.
Catchment and run-off. Water,
        we allow you

your flat roof and rocky bed
but there are also
        tricks we have taught you:
papal fountain, water
feature, liquid chandelier and
    boiling jug. It is, however,
            your own mind

you make up, adept as you are
          – 'the universal solvent' –
at both piecing together
and tearing apart. With or

without us, you find your own
structure, two H's and an O,
               in the infinity

of your three-sidedness, your
     triangulation, at once trinity
and tricycle. Two oars
and a dinghy, rowed.

Colourless, but for
'an inherent hint of blue',
     molecule in which
we are made soluble, the sum
of our water-based parts –

resourceful, exemplary friend
     kindred spirit – not one to jump to
conclusions
as you would traverse a stream, but rather

as you would leap in. Fluid,
by nature – given to swimming more than
being swum –
     with rain as your spokesperson,

tattooed surface of a river's
undiluted wonder,
          snowfall and drift,
you enter the flow

of each of us, turn us around
     as you turn yourself around
as tears,
     sustenance,
          more tears.

4.30pm Cristian told me how, during the latter stages of his childhood, fugitives from the Pinochet regime were sheltered in the family home. A floor had been boarded off for this purpose. For obvious reasons, he and his siblings were never told who was there, or why, or what was going on (although Cristian remembers hearing the sounds of children and, once, a baby crying). He grew up accustomed to unexplained voices inside their family home. It was, he recalled, as if people were living inside the walls.

On drinking water

What besides
pure water a glass
of water contains:

of the sky nothing
necessarily, but always
something

of the cavernous
substratum
calcium, potassium

the wooden ladder we climb
down into the chasm
to swim.

4.45pm During the Pinochet years – that era of disappearances – it was as if the walls started swallowing up the population.

A round, Te Namu

What came of it
went with it

each brilliant young head
polished and balaclava'd

her gaunt team trundlered
and caddied

greenwards. Immovable as she was
at ones and twos, 'all over
                                the park', another

remembered walk
                    down the long aisle, ring-
fenced and spoken for:

Base Hospital, Home Team
here gathered.

Who saw it
coming? An albatross.

An eagle. The golf card following
proceedings. A fleck of earth grassily

sparrowing sunwards
and then the follow-through

the seedlings scattered – that was
us – a kindling

to their own
wilding fires . . .

Her black hair enshadowing
the green, a storm cloud

lingering over the eighteenth
    then moving out

her faraway eyes
even further –
        a clear run home.

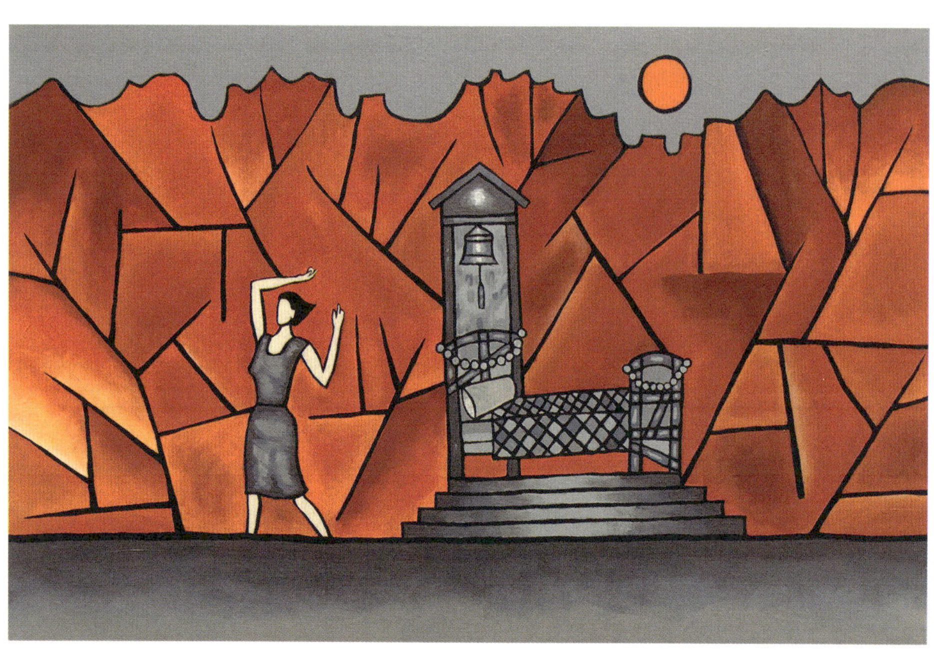

Sombrerería

Men come to me with a headful of this
and that. A hat goes a long way
to making up the mind.

I am often asked what a hat
contains: a lost train
of thought, patch of displaced sky. A well-situated hat can be

many things: ice bucket, dormitory, a nesting place
for the tropic bird, or rocky outcrop of some
distant geography. The hat, I have heard it

said, is a commentary on all that is
wrong with the world. It knows
the true shape of

the head beneath it. Among the racks and boxes
I go a long way
out of my way. Necessarily, the hat completes
          the man, the man

the hat. Wind-resistant
yet weather-dependent, a Panama, Fedora, Porkpie or
Sombrero is not an approximate thing –

it is an island, as a man
is not. With a minute adjustment of the rim
a man becomes a priest

or cowboy or hired killer. Yet there are
certain things a hat refuses to be. A hat is
not a helmet – and, despite being man's

crowning achievement, it is
never a crown. A hat of mine would not stoop
that low. In this windless

hat-friendly town, the world goes past
my window: a pram, a flamenco troupe,
a *coup d'état*. A hat maketh

the man. There is enough inconclusiveness
in the world as it is. Snowlike
my hats fall upon the heads of

the citizens of Santiago. In warm weather
they make themselves
scarce. The moment a stranger

enters my shop, the tilt of his head
tells me where he is from; his hair speaks to me
of wind-flow, humidity, proximity to coast.

Dents, scars and undulations – these
I note – on forehead or temple
or crown. Only this afternoon,

one customer had been struck
by the boom of a yacht, the next scratched
by a low-flying bird –

my guess, a giant owl. Another
had recently encountered
a cupboard door or chandelier. It is these events

that propel men towards my store – the felt hat
offering shelter, protection or, at least
an early warning system.

Homburg or Poor Boy – a hat
consolidates the thinking beneath it.
The innermost lining of a hat

is a man's life. By the time
a customer departs
he has grown to the height of

his hat. Or such is the thinking and so
one day, will be the forgetting.
A thin man is a stem upon which

flowers a tempestuous hat.
My role is that of a baker – a hat
properly fitted, must rise up above

itself. And bear its wearer skywards.
A hat should bring a man to
fullness, fecundity, as the hat itself might be

described as a well-upholstered bird
flightless, except in a Valparaíso southerly.
The shop window a well-fed

multitude. Less contented, the Coquito palm wine
which rampaged through my youth –
the opposite of a hat, it does not clear the head.

Each evening, my hats extend towards
the edges of the city, like taxis or library fines.
Or they reach skywards

above the Santiago Underground
where the hatless dead make what little progress
is allowed them. Broomlike, my gaze

sweeps a man out from under
an ill-suited hat.
In this regard, I am a janitor

a doorman also,
or more correctly a keeper or custodian
of the space within each hat.

The body is a creaking
stairwell spiralling upwards
to this hilltop observatory.

A hat is also an ear
listening in on
the head's business, with the same exactitude

I record the sound of a hat lifting off
and then landing again – I think of myself also
as Air Traffic Control.

A hat is an underlining
of certain things. A hat thrown high
the monkey puzzle tree casts its cool light

upon our feverish brows. Longshoreman
as well as harbourmaster, I am a wearer
of many hats, a man of influence

beyond the polished floors
and racks, these grey banded hats
which lie in wait like battleships

of the Chilean navy – the tall, leaning vessels
of Valparaíso – becalmed yet
hungry for the tumultuous future

as a window full of hats is
for the light of each new day.

for Bruce Foster

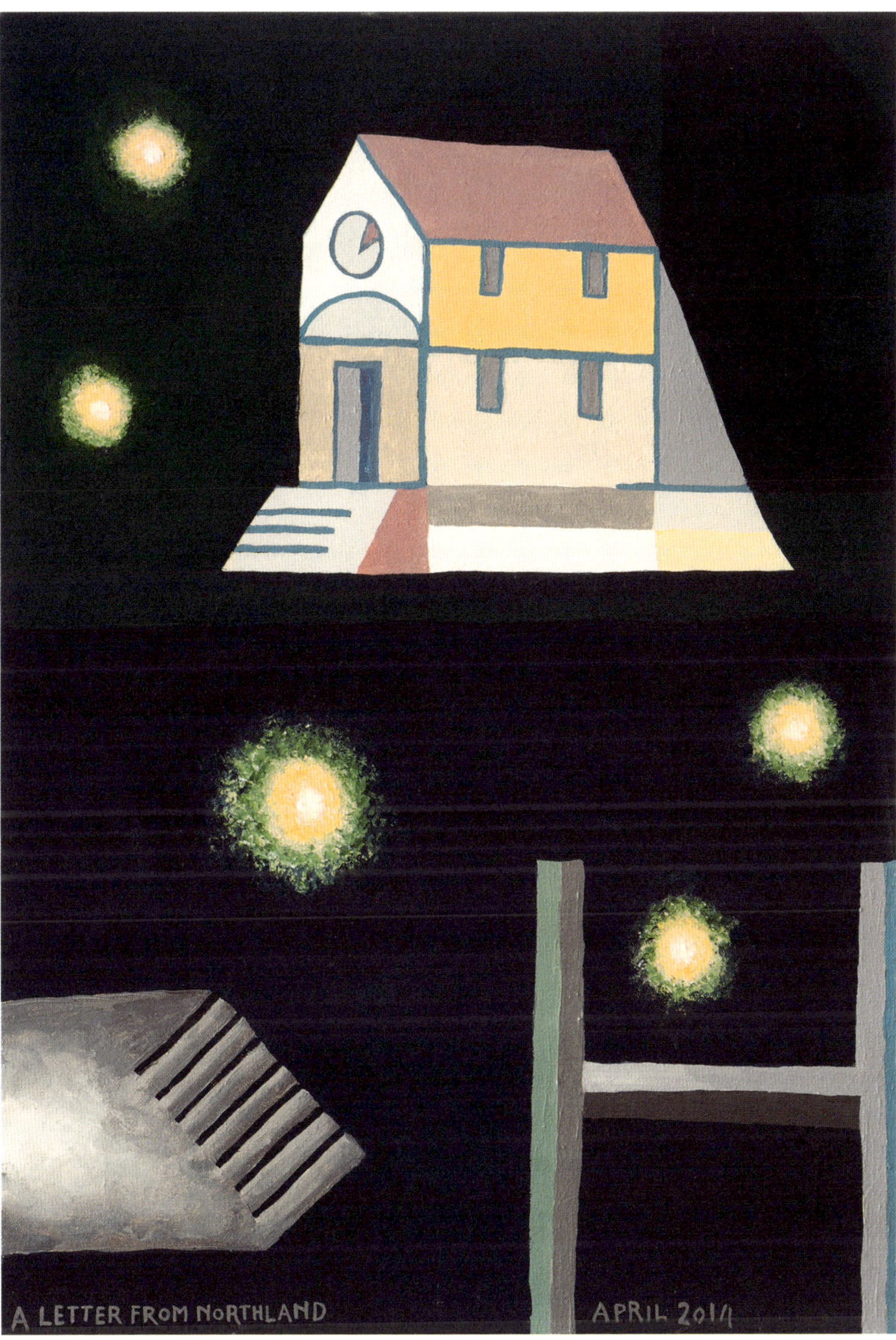
A LETTER FROM NORTHLAND
APRIL 2014

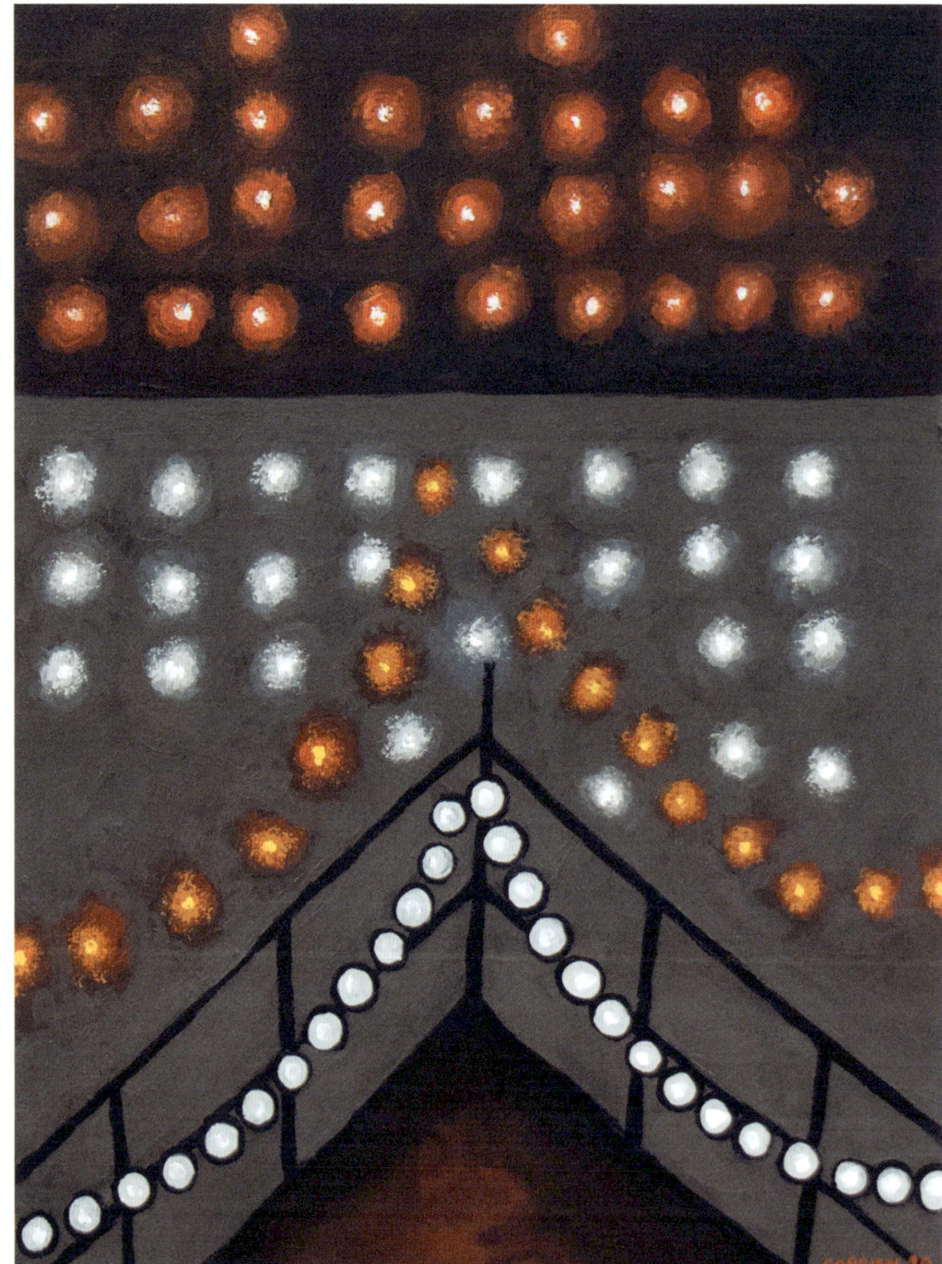

5pm Hovering over the recently constructed wall in the art gallery, from the top of a ladder, Cristian told me that here we had a wall that people could live comfortably inside. A wall that opens out onto the world. A wall that might be a gateway to something new. He then told me a story from his youth concerning a game of tennis he played against his father, the internationally renowned architect Cristian Valdes (senior), in the 1970s – an encounter which directly led to his father inventing what *Architectural Digest* would describe as 'one of the truly great chair designs of the 20th century'.

Cristian's story, which centres on a broken tennis racquet, struck me as a parable for our times – a tale of wreckage and rebirth, a solemn but hopeful note struck for Santiago de Chile as for the city of Christchurch after the earthquakes of 2010 and 2011. His recollection became the basis for a poem titled 'Origin of the Valdes chair'. (He had earlier proposed to me that a tennis net should also be thought of as a kind of wall – a wall based upon the premise that things should go past it, from both directions.)

In a photograph Bruce Foster took of Cristian and me beside the temporary wall in the gallery, it appears we are pretending to play a game of tennis or else rehearsing some inherently joyful dance moves. The wall has led us to a certain loss of inhibition. It has liberated us, momentarily. That was part of the game too, as Cristian related it to me, and part of what the wall had to say.

Origin of the Valdes chair

A game of tennis
          has come to this –

                    a man leans back thirty years
          the long racquet

on the end of his long arm
          as he flips the ball

                    back over the net
          to his father

who volleys. This time, unable
          to get beneath the ball, the boy

                    who is leaning
          thirty years into his future

falls to the ground
          mid-stroke, his racquet exploding

                    in a riot of gut and splintered
          wood. And the game

is over, as is the racquet
          and the father might be about to

                    lose his temper at such
          a deficit of footwork

but instead picks up
          the shattered implement

                    bent around nearly 180 degrees –
          and rotates it, studying

the unlikely mixture
of tension and languor. What to make

of this now? A flowerpot holder, maybe
or stringed instrument

but nothing grows in Santiago
and there are already too many

sad Chilean songs –
what else is an architect to do

but design something. And so
the demolished racquet survives –

outliving the Pinochet regime
Roberto Bolaño

and various tracts of
Valparaíso waterfront –

reborn as a chair
a natural by-product of

a man's leaning backwards
into an abandoned or lost

game. And in the form of which
is contained both easy volley

and impossible return.
Seated thus, a younger

Valdes remembers
his father on the far side of the court

and how it was at that precise moment
the boy became an architect

and today he describes
a house folding backwards

into one freestanding wall
just as, upon its conclusion, a game of tennis

is packed away and all that remains
is the vertical plane

of the net. And he acknowledges his father
in wall, net and racquet.

And in the courtside chair
not far off, observant,
still in the game.

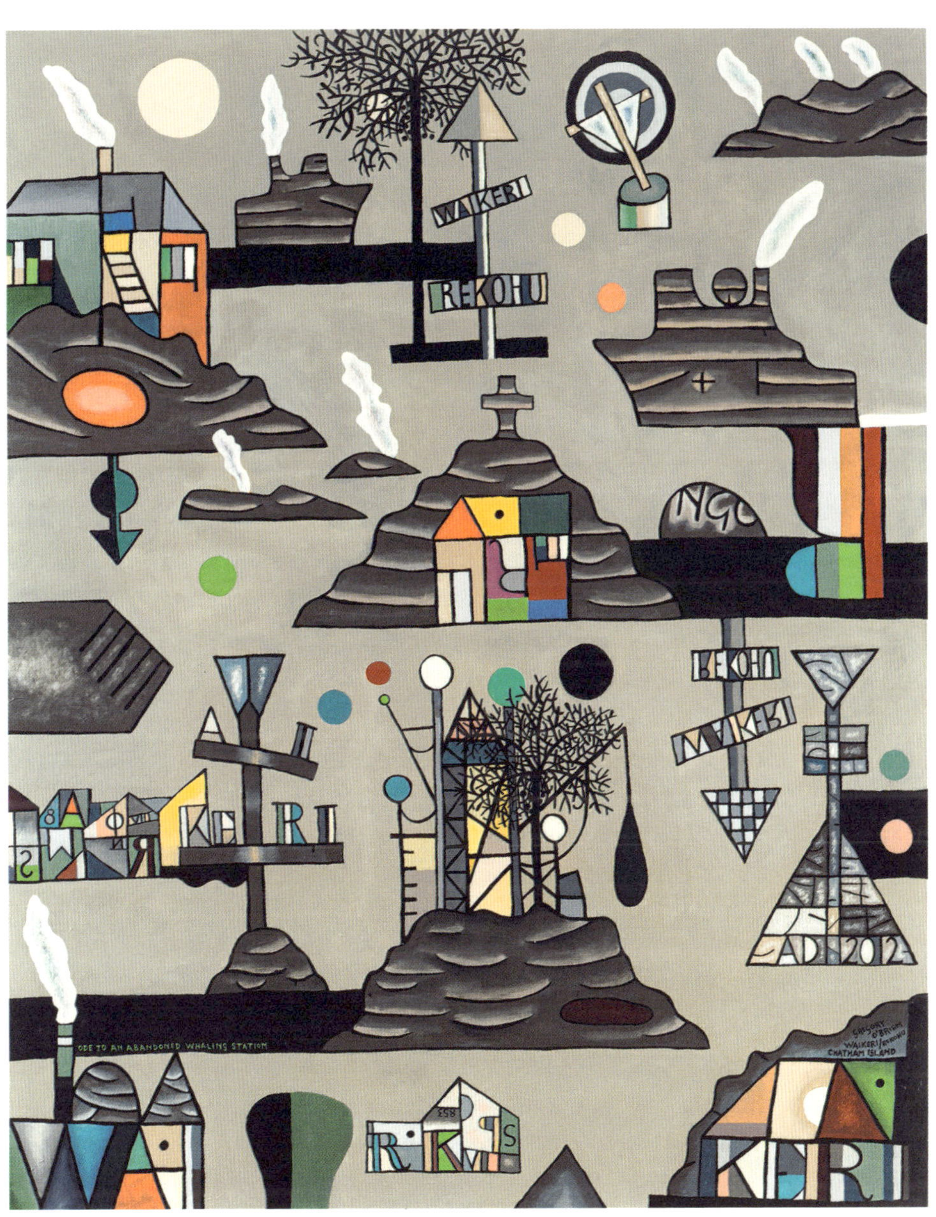
WAIKERI
REKOHU
REKOHU
WAIKERI
AD 2012
ODE TO AN ABANDONED WHALING STATION
GREGORY O'BRIEN
CHATHAM ISLAND

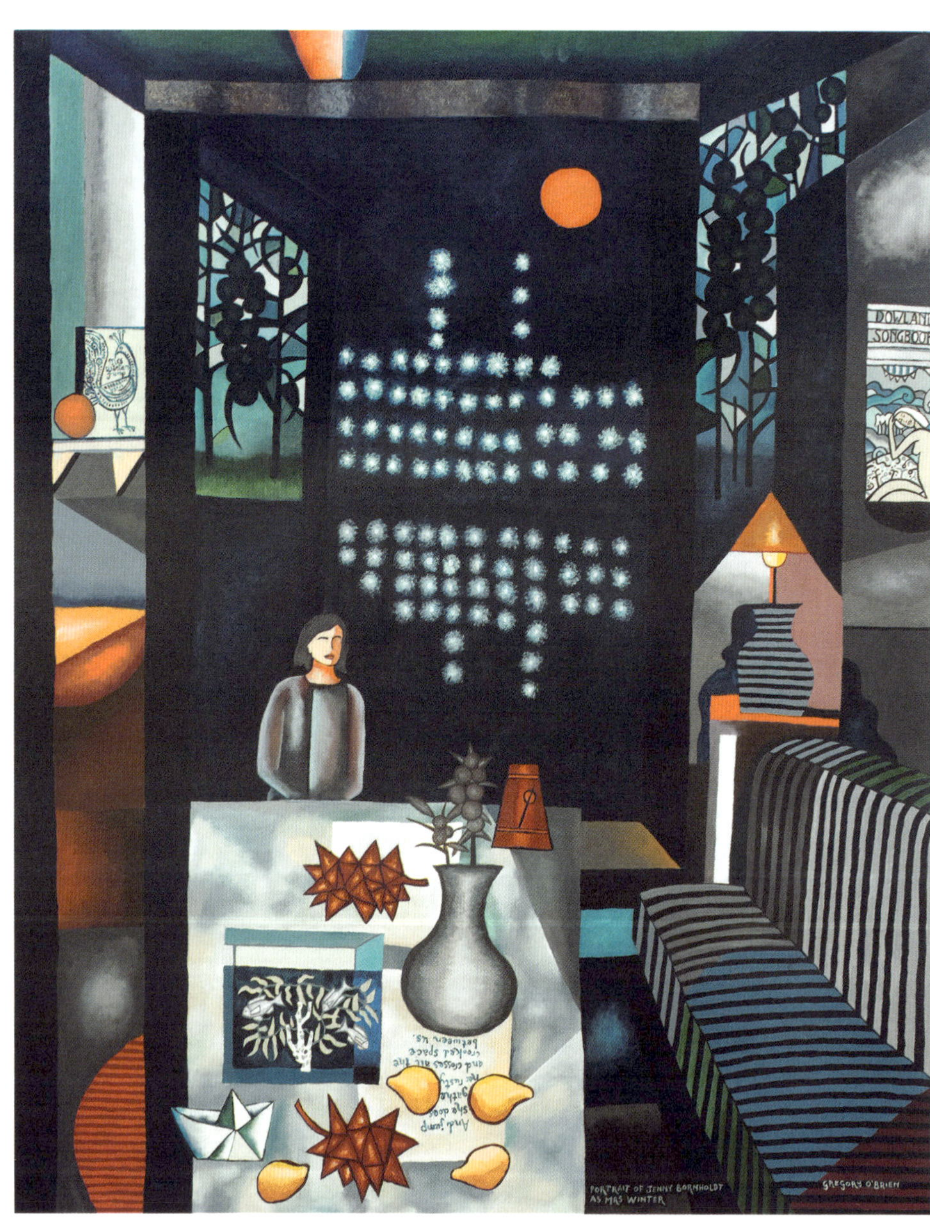

DOWLAND
SONGBOOK
And jump
she does
her rusty
and crosses all the
crooked space
between us.
PORTRAIT OF JENNY BORNHOLDT
AS MRS WINTER
GREGORY O'BRIEN

For Jen at Three O'Clock

With us, ice melt and low land
fog, creaking thornbush,

sandarac and walnut lawn. With us
towers and minarets

of the asparagus field, each blink
and muffled cough, each

recitation and
resuscitation, mountain

torrent and gasping stream. The track
from Horseshoe

to Fiddler's Flat, and the round trip
via Home Hills Runs Road, with us

and upon us, these days on earth, and
against us the possibility

of elsewhere. A layering of
piripiri, gentian,

with us, a rare climbing moss,
only us.

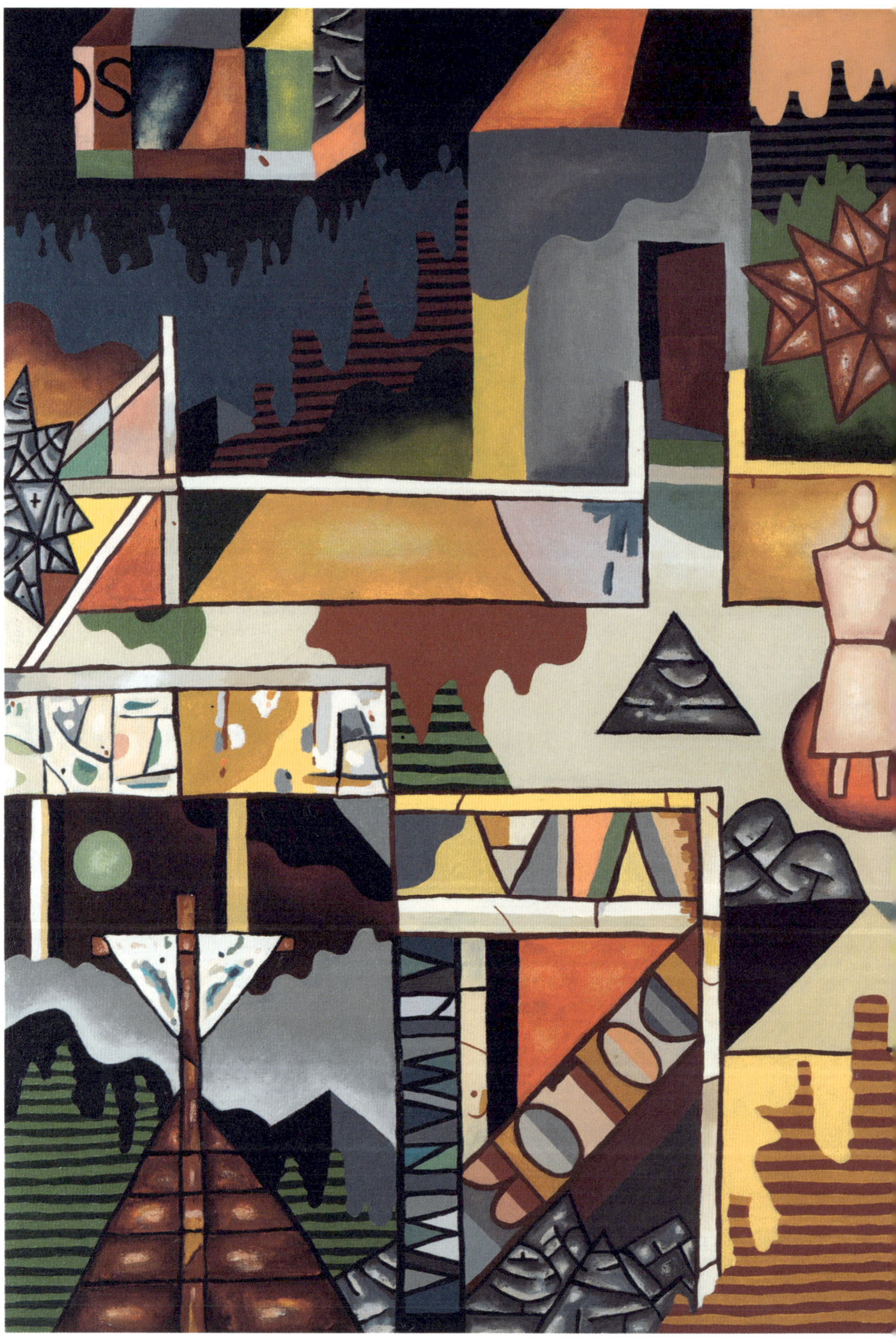
OS

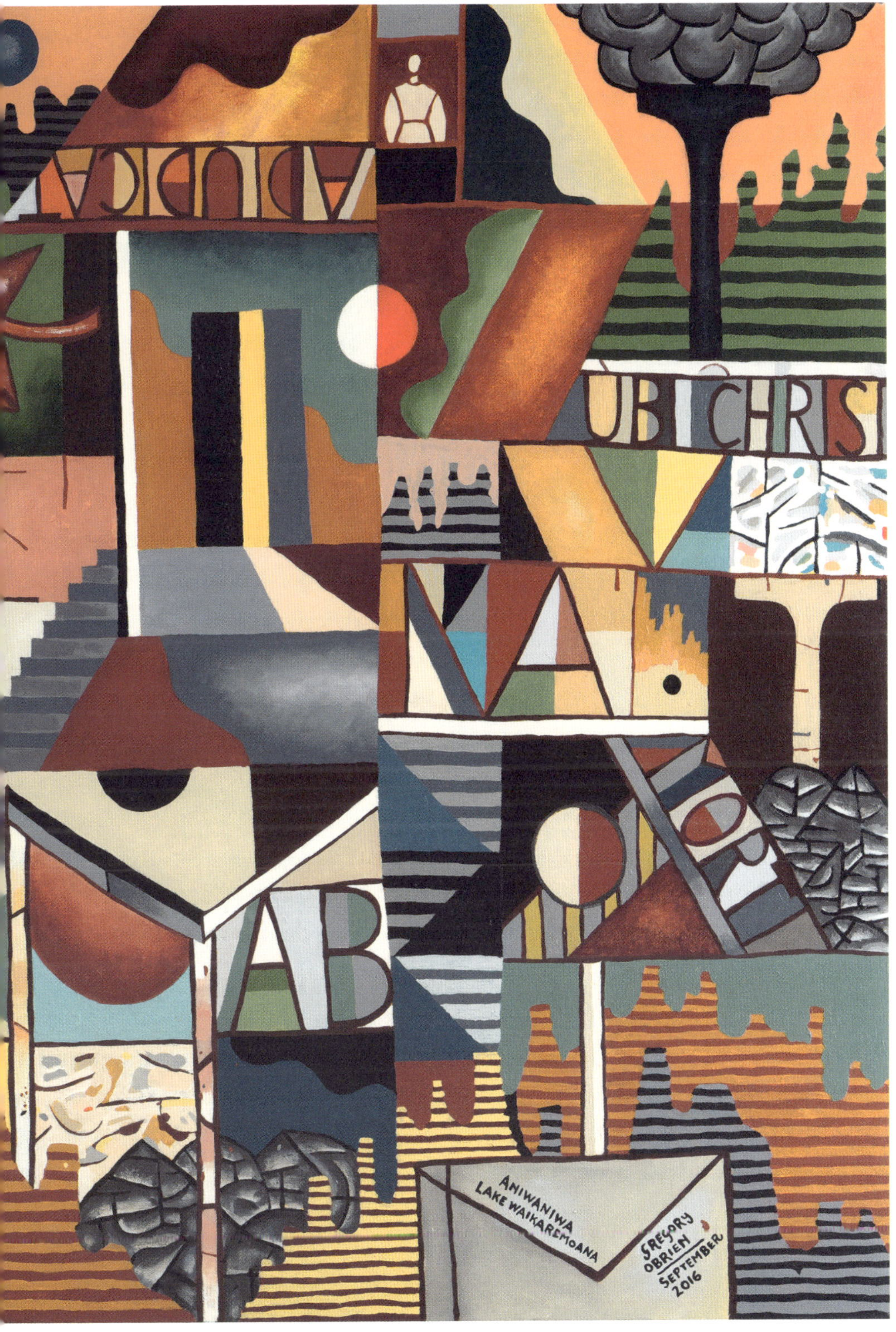
UBI CHRIS
ANIWANIWA
LAKE WAIKAREMOANA
GREGORY
OBRIEN
SEPTEMBER
2016

NOTES TO ACCOMPANY THE POEMS AND PAINTINGS

What is this particular brightness we expect of poetry? And on what or whose account? If the times are dark, oppressive, tunnel-like – as they seem presently – maybe poetry can be a lantern. Or a firefly, or the glowing bud of a cigarette on a dark night. But for poetry to be these things it can't simply reflect its times – it has to radiate on its own terms, within and beyond that darkness. It is poetry's job to flicker and glow and, with luck, emit some mysterious luminescence. At times I feel those are its only real criteria.

In the past I've used drawings or paintings to illuminate poetry. And I've used poetry to converse with, and maybe shed light upon, painted images. This book gathers these two endeavours in a co-equal arrangement. While the words and paintings echo and overlap, and occasionally coincide, the paintings are not illustrations. On the other hand, the poems are neither explanations of, nor elaborations upon, the paintings.

Many of these poems and paintings are rooted in specific places – Santiago de Chile, Alexandra, Niue, Meretoto . . . 'Three O'Clock' in the title of the final poem, is the name of a settlement – now deserted – in Central Otago. For the most part, however, the poems were worked and reworked away from their place of origin – the present writer's notebook and desktop are their truest address. Bearing that in mind, the ordering of poems in this collection has less to do with their geographical referents and more to do with colour, tone, phrasing or maybe a faint thematic thread. The poems and paintings also share compositional tendencies, an inclination towards the layering of images, an amiable – for the most part – interplay of elements. The two paintings at the front of the book offer, I would suggest, a template for much of what follows.

The title *House & Contents* implies an insurance policy, but against what? Reading back through the poems, I'm struck by the temporary nature of much of their architecture – the variously pitched tents, the demolished John Scott building at Aniwaniwa, the hat store in Santiago now only a memory. Maybe this book is itself another kind of architectural proposition – a structure inside of which these houses, those extant and otherwise, have been rebuilt.

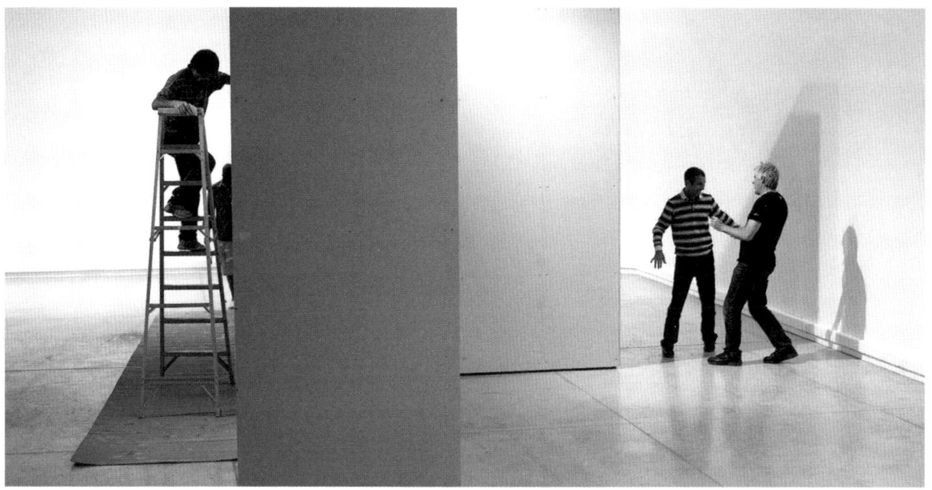

Author (far right), architect and temporary wall, Santiago 2013 (see p. 95).
PHOTOGRAPH BY BRUCE FOSTER

ACKNOWLEDGEMENTS

Many of these poems have appeared previously. My thanks to the editors of the following publications: *Sport, New Zealand Books, Jaam, Christchurch Art Gallery Bulletin* (NZ); *Poetry Chicago, Harvard Review* (USA); *Cyphers* (Ireland); *Gutter* (Scotland); *PN Review, Warwick Review, Manchester Review* (UK). Some have appeared in the Pear Tree Press publications *8 Poems 2019* and *8 Poems 2021*, on Paula Green's Poetry Shelf website and the online *Best New Zealand Poems*. 'Sombrerería', 'Great age of machines' and 'Origin of the Valdes chair' first appeared in the chapbook *Citizen of Santiago* (Wellington: Trapeze, 2014) with photographs by Bruce Foster. Others appeared in *Mannix & Culhane* (Adelaide: Lil Esther Books, 2018) with drawings by Ken Bolton, and in *Eight Poems from the Henderson House* (with Jenny Bornholdt), handprinted by the indefatigable Brendan O'Brien. 'Beach house' appeared in *Black Barn – portrait of a place* (Auckland: Godwit, 2017). The quotation from Hugh MacDiarmid on p. 34 is from *Selected Poetry*, ed. Alan Riach and Michael Grieve, Manchester: Carcanet, 1992. Used with permission of the publisher. An earlier version of 'House and contents' was published as 'A quaking of smallish things' in *PN Review* 216, March–April 2014. I acknowledge the warm-hearted support granted my poetry and visual art by *PN Review* editor Michael Schmidt over the past three decades. 'On drinking water' appeared in a catalogue accompanying Euan Macleod's exhibition *High Water* at Watters Gallery, Sydney, in 2018. 'Paula Rego' appeared in the tribute book *Paula*, ed. Anthony Rudolf, on the occasion of the artist's eightieth birthday.

The paintings in this book were produced between 2014 and 2020. Thanks to Jenny Neligan and Penney Moir at Bowen Galleries for ongoing support, and to Barbara Speedy at The Diversion, Picton. I'm also grateful to the following: Andrew and Penny Gawith (who commissioned the two Matukituki Valley paintings), Bronwen Golder, John Gow and Fiona Taylor, Campbell McLachlan and Rhona Fraser, Martine Tait, Jane Connor, Nick Bevin, Mark Smith, David Straight, Nigel and Marie Brown and to Reuben Friend of Pātaka Art + Museum, Porirua. Some poems and paintings included in the exhibitions *Wai / Water* and *The Water Project* toured to the Ashburton Art Gallery, Canterbury Museum, Aratoi Museum of Art and History (Wairarapa),

Pātaka Art + Museum, Suter Art Gallery (Nelson), Sarjeant Art Gallery (Whanganui) and were exhibited as part of the Festival of Colour in Wanaka, 2019. For further information visit www.thewaterprojectnz.org.

I'm grateful to the Henderson Arts Trust for time spent in Alexandra, Central Otago, in 2018 and subsequently. Special thanks to Grahame and Fiona Sydney, and to all the others listed in 'Te whakarite puāwai'. Many of the paintings in this book were included in the touring exhibition, *The Wading Birds of Drybread – Paintings by Gregory O'Brien 2016–2020*, which was shown at Eastern Southland Art Gallery, Central Stories Art Gallery and Museum (Alexandra), Ashburton Art Gallery and Millennium Gallery (Blenheim). Thanks to the staff of those institutions, in particular Jim and Marcella Geddes, Shirin Khosraviani and Cressida Bishop. Thanks also to ongoing collaborators: John Pule, Bruce Foster, Elizabeth Thomson, Robin White, Ken Bolton, Euan Macleod, Noel McKenna and Michael Kempson.

Thanks to old and new friends who helped this book along its way – to Elizabeth Caffin, and the team at AUP: Sam Elworthy, Katharina Bauer, Sophia Broom and Lauren Donald; to proofreader Louise Belcher; to designer Keely O'Shannessy; and to the home-team, Jen, Jack-Marcel, Felix and Carlo.

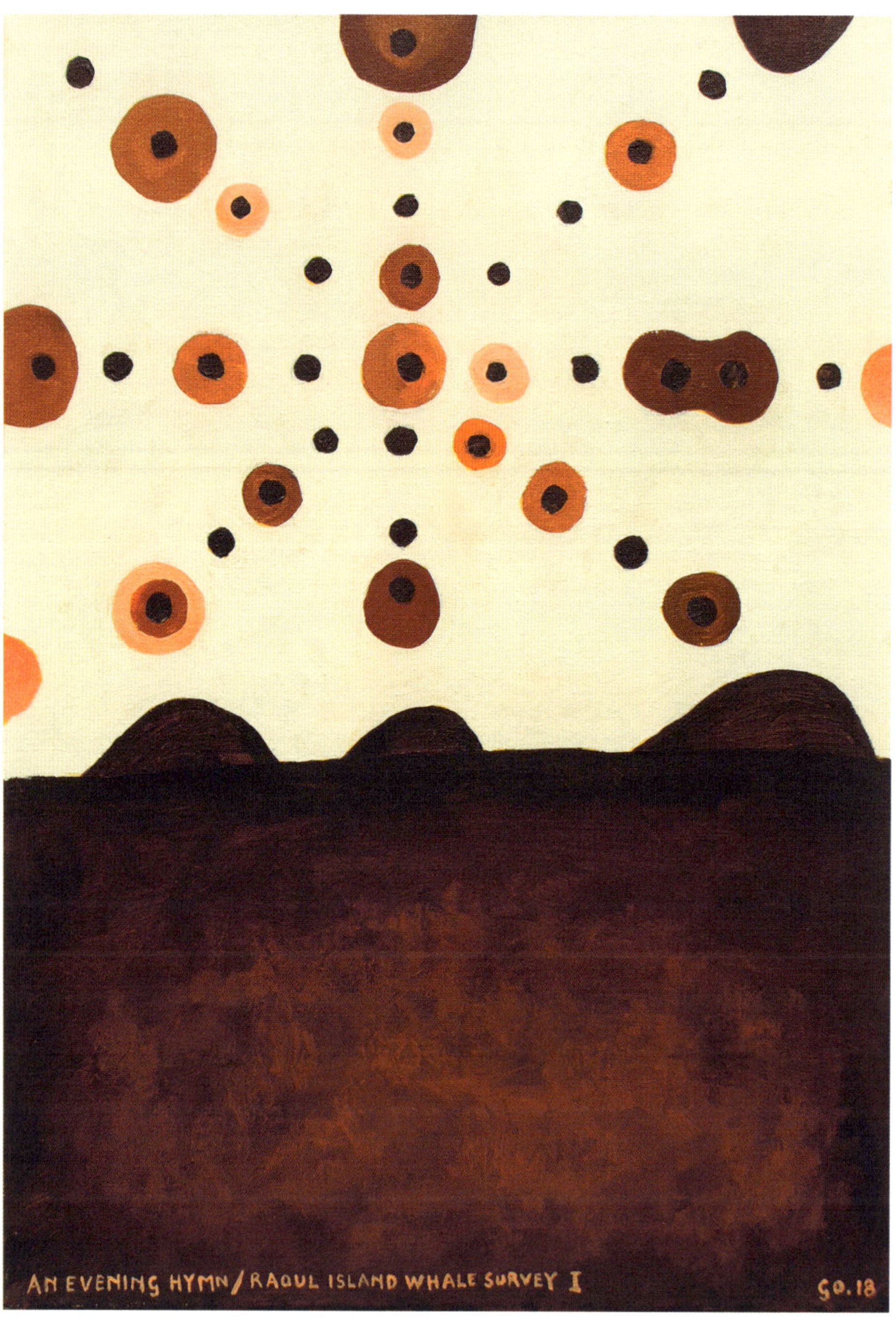
AN EVENING HYMN / RAOUL ISLAND WHALE SURVEY I
GO.18

CONTENTS

I. Poems

II. Paintings

First published 2022
Auckland University Press
University of Auckland
Private Bag 92019
Auckland 1142
New Zealand
www.aucklanduniversitypress.co.nz

ISBN 978 1 86940 964 7

A catalogue record for this book is available from the National Library of New Zealand

Book design by Keely O'Shannessy
Paintings photographed by Stephen A'Court, Bruce Foster, Shirin Khosraviani, Mark Smith and Mike Wilkinson

This book was printed on FSC® certified paper

Printed in China by Everbest Printing Investment Ltd